WHAT POETS ARE

UP AND DOWN *with the* WRITING LIFE

LIKE

GARY SOTO

SASQUATCH BOOKS
SEATTLE

To Loving Carolyn
Who Has Seen It All

Printed in the United States of America

Published by Sasquatch Books
17 16 15 14 13   9 8 7 6 5 4 3 2 1

Editor: Gary Luke
Project editor: Michelle Hope Anderson
Design: Anna Goldstein
Cover illustration: Frida Clements
Copy editor: Michael Townley

Library of Congress Cataloging-in-Publication
Data is available.

ISBN: 978-1-57061-874-1

Sasquatch Books
1904 Third Avenue, Suite 710
Seattle, WA 98101
(206) 467-4300
www.sasquatchbooks.com
custserv@sasquatchbooks.com

SUSTAINABLE FORESTRY INITIATIVE

Certified Chain of Custody
Promoting Sustainable Forestry
www.sfiprogram.org
SFI-01268

SFI label applies to the text stock

ACKNOWLEDGMENTS

SEVERAL OF THESE PIECES appeared in the literary magazines *Huizache*, the *Threepenny Review*, and *Zyzzyva*.

"Though We Started Out New," "Don't Do It," and "Fable of the Lost Poets" were published as the chapbook *The Three of Us* by Aureole Press at the University of Toledo. The fine-press printer was Tim Geiger.

"The Wind Sends Small Creatures" and "At Rest, Laborers Lean on Me" appeared in *The Word Exchange: Anglo-Saxon Poems in Translation* (W. W. Norton & Company, 2011), edited by Greg Delanty and Michael Matto.

The poet greatly appreciates Peter Fong, Gary Luke, and Carolyn Soto for editorial suggestions.

ACKNOWLEDGMENTS

PREFACE

AGING POETS ARE LIKE cartons of milk just days away from expiration, when they become the curdled contents ready to be poured down the drain. This is what a poet friend of mine reflected at the end of the school year. I argued, "No, old verbal prankster, not every poet—I'm a slender quart of skim milk while you, I'm afraid, are a squat carton of half-and-half." We love this kind of banter though we remain best of friends. Still, he might be right on one score: age does tend to make one sour. He occasionally goes off on this train of thought with a proper drink in his paw, reminiscing "Oh, those poems, those publications, those nearly grasped pearly prizes and honors, those bookstore readings, those fellowships that allowed us to travel." Those bookstore readings? I recall more empty chairs than occupants, and some in those chairs were just resting before they shoved off to the magazine section.

That there's more hair circling our ears than on top of our heads is a concern. A headier worry is that many of our best poems have already been written and now lay in the past. What poems do we have left in us? I have thirteen books of poetry for adults along with seven for young readers. I began writing poetry at age twenty while a junior college student, with a vague notion of what a poem was and what a poem should do emotionally. How did I start? By discovering Edward Field's poem "Unwanted," in which a meek man desperately seeks recognition, even if it means hanging his photo on a bulletin board in the post office. As a teen, the speaker in the poem had been bullied and ignored. He suffered slurs—"dumbbell, good-for-nothing, jewboy . . . sissy." Now in his mid-thirties, his once curly hair is fuzzy. He has no physique. His eyesight has diminished. In short, he is the archetype of a pushover. But he has one meaningful attribute: he responds to love. If you call him, he, like a happy dog, will come. How I leaked a tear or two and said in my heart, "Mr. Field, you are recognized."

Though I discovered poetry in 1972, I had the emotional stirrings of a poet earlier on—much earlier, at age four, when I had sympathy for a bean plant that had to live with its tiny arms outstretched, as if being punished, like Jesus on the cross. I didn't have much in the way of toys, so pinto beans served as my army men. They worked nicely as I moved them across the sandy ground of our house on Braly Street. One morning I discovered that a bean plant suddenly had emerged, unraveling to its full height. I was awed by its appearance and then bewildered when within days the arms of the plant began to lower, dehydrated. Then another bean plant appeared, and then others, all of them first lifting their arms and then lowering them, their lung-shaped leaves wilting under the Fresno heat. At age four I grasped the circle of life.

These prose pieces have the mystery of poetry—brief, imagistic, true, reflective, and individually mine. I write about like-minded souls, seventeenth-century diarist Samuel Pepys, for instance, and offer light moments such as the time I rubbed shoulders with Hayley Mills, child star of the early 1960s. I write about London and Fresno, and Berkeley, where I have lived for thirty-five years. I'm a scoundrel on some pages and a noble on others. I write about poet friends—Christopher Buckley, Jon Veinberg, Gary Young—and another amigo, David Ruenzel. My wife of thirty-eight years is with me in these pages. My arms that once lifted skyward are now at my side, exhausted.

I'm a poet, though possibly better dressed than most of them, as readers will discover in "The Winning Crowd." I'm greedy, generous, jealous, occasionally drunk, educated in a quirky way, overlooked, witty, and team member not. I live by my five senses, partic-ularly taste—"God, I love that wine—can I get it for under ten bucks?"

I've been writing poetry for forty years—this is what I do. I pulled Fame's longish hair and discovered her wearing a wig—the locks came off in my hand. I'm troubled, then not troubled. I believe in the greatness of Pablo Neruda. I believe in ignored artists, such as DeLoss McGraw. I appreciate gardens, literary history, and novels that I can read in three days. My favorite color is yellow, though for years I thought it was blue. I support California Rural Legal Assistance. My heroes are members of the Lincoln Brigade. The 442nd Regimental Combat Team also means something to me. Cesar Chavez is a flag in my heart. My daughter Mariko is smarter than I. I love my wife. My cat adores me from any distance.

I'm a poet who feels like all the others—mostly ignored. I work best in the morning. My mail arrives in late afternoon. Dogs appear frequently in my poems. I respond to love. If you call me, I will get up from my chair, a little slower now that I'm a senior, and come to you.

AGING POET

I CANCELLED MY LOVE FOR THE DOG when he yawned while I was reciting a poem. He yawned a second time before I got to the really good part, rose stiffly from his rug, and squeezed his bulk through the cat door. This departure demonstrated his dislike of poetry. Or was it only my poetry? Was I losing it? Still, I wasn't about to give up on poetry—or on the white-haired muse who, after my thirty-seven-year career, no longer appears to have much bite. (I can imagine her depositing her teeth in a jar, just before sleep.) At the fruit bowl, I lifted a fig, pierced it with my fingers, then ate it with my eyes closed. It was the best sex I'd had in months. I was enjoying a second, drier fig when a tomcat slinked by the window, feathers from a hot meal still in his mouth. I know this cat. The furry beast has deflowered many a young cat and fathered many a kitten. He eats birds with a toothy fervor, until only the heads and feet are left.

The late afternoon fell, another inky thumbprint at the edge of my poem. The dog returned through the cat door. It was my fault. I'd had him neutered when he was a lollygagging pup. Now old, he holds a tennis ball in his mouth, waiting for someone to play with.

I know the feeling.

AT THE POET'S REST HOME, on a country road in Madera County, I don't have much to do. I count trucks that rattle down the road, jackrabbits that scoot through brush, and the occasional coyote with a burnt-tipped snout. It's 2034. The dog I recited poetry to is gone, and so is the tomcat, my wife, and my friends, halos around their heads and, for those with musical talents, harps in their laps. With a large kindergarten pencil, I keep busy filling in sudoku books, bought in bulk. I pet the dust from a potted plant. I watch television and fart into cushions. I drape my grayish underwear on a radiator, flags of surrender. I tap my finger on the arm of a recliner. I get up and touch a novel on the shelf: the writer is dead. I touch another book, whose author published six volumes of poetry, three translations, and one unreadable work of criticism—he's really dead. I touch the warped spine of a poetry book: she died while reaching for a can of salsa on the top shelf—or so it was rumored.

I sleep and I wake, as now. But I have at least one duty, which is to raise the kitchen blinds by tugging a rope. Unsatisfied, I do this over and over: I can't get the hem of the blinds at just the right level. I pause, frustrated. The morning sun is fierier than ever before.

Sloppy me, I never could do my chores right. I tried to speak truth to the small, such as children sucking on the barrels of toy guns, and to well-fed oldsters, such as bankers with their hearing aids turned off. I was a poet with a shiny silver pen. I was made of flesh and words, not a marketable talent, such as the ability to raise rafters in new subdivisions. I wasn't a handyman with a tool belt at my waist. I could rake leaves, prune rosebushes, and clean gutters with a screwdriver. But look at me now! I can't get the blinds straight, crooked things! My fingers are pale as the underside of a starfish. This is how I sail the last of my hours, tugging the blinds up and down, never getting them just right.

SELF-IMPROVEMENT

WHAT I REALLY NEED IS a deeper education, one where I can open the top of my head and throw in a lot of books. I plan to reread *The Discoverers* by Daniel J. Boorstin, the popular historian, and to reset my mind so that it dwells not on contemporary problems (such as poems rejected from Midwest magazines no one has ever heard about), but on the concerns of a time when my distant relative, the Neanderthal man, was foraging along the Danube. I have every belief that education straightens the spine and provides novel ways of looking at shit. Education leads to jobs and job creation—O the stimulation of a steady job.

I mean to study, like a scholar, and brush up on the cradle of civilization, namely the Euphrates River and Fertile Crescent. The erudition I want calls for a brow-furrowed interest in myths, the mysterious source of the Nile, algebra as founded by Persian eggheads, contraptions devised by Archimedes, and the wheeling stars at night—is that a bear or a bear driving a chariot? But when it comes to the common man, I hesitate. I fear getting to know my ancestors—hell, I don't even like my current relatives. Why multiply misery by acquainting myself with even crueler lowbrows?

This spring I will commit myself to light verse about a tulip. I will speak for the anthills and transient possums dressed in pajamas. I will consider what my wife says: "Gary, you have to be nicer." There is time for this, time for war with the Spanish subjunctive, and time to become a master gardener. I'll rake a trowel over a plot of earth. Tomatoes will grow in full sunlight, along with chilies and cilantro, ancestors worth knowing.

THE RIGHT ANSWER

WHEN FRANK LLOYD WRIGHT was in court (a business venture gone wrong), he was asked to state his occupation. He answered without hesitation, "I'm the greatest architect in America." Later, a flabbergasted friend asked, "How could you have said that about yourself?" Wright might have been leaving the court, his famously broad-brimmed hat in hand, a smirk on his face—a smirk which, like the clip-clop of his brogues against inferior marble, registered the mediocrity of the courthouse. Outlandish conjecture on my part, perhaps, but it might have happened; he might have turned and shrugged before issuing his reply. Whatever the setting, his answer has entered the record: "Why, I was under oath, wasn't I?" In short, he could not tell a lie. Later he judged himself in another way: "Early in life I had to choose between honest arrogance and hypocritical humility. I chose arrogance."

To posture in such manner is not possible for us, the legion of poets, we who are unemployed, or underpaid when employed, we who nibble eraser heads for a little creative energy. We wouldn't dare announce in court: "I am the best poet in the country." Or, "The best poet west of the Mississippi." Or even, "West of the Colorado River at high tide."

While we may speak of our talents as image-makers, at heart we bards are full of doubt. We wonder: "Why am I making myself poor by writing poetry?" We lack confidence, though we may bray to others that we're kick-ass versifiers. Note this: We don't wear broad-brimmed hats.

FISHING FOR A POEM

LET'S DO GEOGRAPHY HERE, local history as well. The Fresno River is a seasonal rivulet of chemical-tainted runoff where the fish have reinvented themselves as frogs, lizards, and other squirmy creatures. Or so I exaggerate. But the river is undeniably scented with effluent from farms and dairies. And I don't exaggerate when I report that no fisherman has seen the river between June and October. In those months it's bone dry. Tumbleweeds roll across it, blown both by nature's wind and the wind of traffic from Highway 99. But come late fall this tributary of small importance does fill and move as rivers like to do. Geese will stop and bathe in that dank brew.

Rivers make poets dream. Rivers make us long for adventure.

Once, after a hard spring rain, I hiked along the Fresno River and found a poet friend fishing on its sandy banks. His beard was the color of tumbleweed, with the texture of tumbleweed—spiky and mean. My friend C. was not mean, however, but as good-hearted as Whitman, louder than Whitman, rough like Whitman. His face was lined from the sun and from the action of breaking into laughter. A storyteller, he was a musty fellow with dark stains on his shirt. His Levis were oilslick from mounting and dismounting his hog of a Harley motorcycle.

C. was old as trees, as fossils, as the dust and sparks chipped from rocks. As a wandering troubadour, he'd witnessed a burning bush, manna falling from the sky, a red sea parting like a huge zipper—old is what I mean. We could have sat opposite each other, C. on one side of this narrow and shallow river, me on the other side. Neither of us would've been in competition, except for a fish foolish enough to bite, wiggle weakly on the line, and end up as the smallest trophy hanging on the wall of the downstairs den.

CONCERT

WHILE MY WIFE WAS ON VACATION with college girlfriends (Egypt before the revolution), I did my best to keep busy. For me, busyness meant theater, classical music concerts, and beery blues venues. The first concert was at Holy Names University in Oakland, in a dimly lit sanctuary with pulsating hearts of votive candles. Although the concert was advertised as free, there was a basket perched near a font at the entrance. I peered in: ones and fives, tens and twenties—a sliding scale, it appeared. For me it was wait and see.

I found a seat in the front row. As I was alone— meaning without a companion—I read the two-sided program of the 43rd Anniversary Kodály Center Choral

Concert several times. By summer light through stained-glass windows I read that Holy Names University is the oldest center for Kodály-based education.

"Kodály," I muttered. "Kodály, Kodály . . ."

I discovered that this method of instruction was devised by Hungarian composer and educator Zoltán Kodály, 1882–1967. His approach placed music (choral, I assumed) at the center of a child's upbringing. The curriculum was available in many languages and, thus, in many countries—even, possibly, in Egypt, where my wife and her girlfriends would be riding camels. (This conjecture reflects my understanding of that country, along with an image of pyramids so bright with sunlight that a pair of sunglasses is required to appreciate them properly.) On the program, there was a telephone number if you wanted to know more about Kodály.

The concert would include works by Koechlin, Bárdos, Hassler, Ligeti, and di Lasso (never heard of them). The conductor was László Matos of Hungary, an honorable-sounding name. The choral group—sopranos, altos, tenors, baritones, basses—numbered over forty. Because I didn't want to look like a lonely old man with nothing to do, I read energetically, marching my finger down the roster, doing a rough count, even imagining their ethnic breakdown. I was, in fact, completing the count when the choral group marched in, single file, all smiling, each with a black binder. The conductor followed—maestro Matos in tails—which had us, the audience of forty or so, clapping with appreciative heat. The maestro bowed, then said—in halting English that suggested English wasn't his first language, nor his second (Europeans are by nature more adept at languages)—that it was an honor to be conducting that evening's concert.

The first piece was by Scarlatti (heard of him); he was followed by the composers of unknown origin. Then it was back to Scarlatti, and on to two haunting selections by Liszt, including "Salve Regina."

It was during a piece by Luis de Victoria that one of the sopranos collapsed in a faint, her neck snapping backward when she hit the carpeted floor, face down. I was in the front row, and I rushed to her aid, knelt, and thought, Now what? I considered propping her into a sitting position, then remembered from God-knows-what television program that I could do more damage than good if her neck was injured. Still, I risked rolling her over—or trying to roll her, as she was tall and big-boned, though not large, not a woman in, as I've heard it described, "full swing." One hand found her hip (had to get a good grip), the other a shoulder packed with muscle. With effort, I rolled her like a sack of grain. A person behind me fanned her with a program. More than two others suggested that we should take her arms and pull her up—a sensible next move.

So that's what we did—a big-bellied baritone and me, scarecrow of a poet—each on one arm. As we slowly raised her up, her head tilted to the left, then the right, only regaining the center when she came to. She appeared drugged. Her hair covered her eyes. She blinked and fanned the hair away. With our aid she got to her feet, one foot feeling around for the pump that had become dislodged. Two sopranos led her away, through a door near the altar. There was a murmur of relief from both chorus and audience. After a few minutes, the chorus reassembled and cleared their throats, whispering to one another about what had made Claire faint—her name was Claire.

At intermission I floated a twenty into the basket, fully satisfied with the unfamiliar music in my ears. My heart raced. I had something new to do. While I couldn't equate my actions with medicine, I did think that they helped me more than they helped Claire.

I went home, windshield wipers clacking in drizzle, and wrote a poem.

THE OAKLAND ZOO

I LINGERED IN FRONT OF THE CHIMP'S CAGE, having had enough of the motionless elephant and the clacking of the toucan's beak—the bird was hidden behind leaves, as if on a veiled audition. The frantic pace of the wolverine was unnerving. The llamas chewing cud made me want to shout, "OK, fella, swallow." The bear slept. The peacock dragged his ballroom gown across pebbles. The rhino was knee-deep in his leaf-strewn pond with a freeloading pelican on his wrinkled back.

Now I was facing a lone chimp—a representative from those picking lice in the corner? He had strolled over with his chimp gait. Instead of pushing a begging hand at me, his small, whiskery face showed worry. Had he heard that a major publisher had showed me the door?

"Chimp," I said in my heart, "I once wrote a story about your kind lost on a raft—Noah had pulled up anchor and you poor swimmers were trying to catch up." He wouldn't have known that, of course. Included in a book called *Help Wanted*, the story appears to be unknown to everyone except me and the publisher.

I was moody. I had walked through a dark cloud of rejection—not rejection per se, but the absence of response to my manuscripts. The company hadn't said goodbye by telephone, e-mail, or letter. It hadn't even let me go with the secondhand smoke of rumor. After a twenty-year relationship, Harcourt—now Houghton Mifflin Harcourt—simply refused to acknowledge me. I had come full circle, the merry-go-round of success had slowed to a stop. It was time to get off my high horse and saddle up a burro.

The chimp rattled the fence. He offered a smile, teeth crooked as dice, and gestured with his hand—no, with a finger. From the end of this digit, he offered me a dab of moist snot. Was this a delicacy in the primate world? He stretched his arm through the fence, as far as it would reach. I shamefully stepped back. He, in turn, withdrew his arm. Were his feelings hurt? Or was he just teasing me? He tasted the snot, ate it with gusto, then pushed his finger back into his nose. Somewhere, in another cage, a water buffalo was snorting. The toucan continued to clack its beak. When the peacock cried, a chevron of birds hit the sky.

I looked back at the chimp and smiled. His offer was one of the nicest I'd received in a long time.

MY TIME WITH
KURT VONNEGUT

NEW YORK CITY, the 1985 Modern Language Association Conference. Cold weather gripped the streets, and six Latino writers, me among them, on a collapsible stage, hollered to mostly empty chairs how we couldn't find any big-time publishers. We hollered. We exclaimed that our only outlets were small presses that turned out stapled jobs on kitchen tables. In my heart, though, I was thinking that—for this company of writers, myself included—the trick to publication was better writing. One of the participants barked like Fidel, fist in the air, inspiring fear in me, at least. He was heavy and on the end of the stage. Would the weight of his anger catapult us into the air? I had a momentary vision of us piled atop one another. Funny, I thought, very funny. I was smirking privately at this image when a silent Kurt Vonnegut tiptoed into the large room. He looked around for about fifteen seconds. He could see that nothing was happening. Then his famous face became distorted with confusion. Had he realized that he was in the wrong room? Was he disagreeing with our rants? Or agreeing? He departed while a buddy of mine was telling the chairs how he had done a reading at a library in Texas and the stupid librarian had misspelled his Aztec name.

I never saw Mr. Vonnegut again.

THE BERKELEY LIBRARY

A VOICE ASKED NONE TOO QUIETLY, "Why you dressed that way?" I was third in line to check out books—a biography of Genet, a guide to Ireland, an oversized book on African beadwork for my wife—when this voice and its wind of unpleasantness provoked me to lean away.

I was dressed in wool slacks and a cashmere sweater. My shoes were Italian loafers, not trainers or flip-flops. When I turned, I discovered a man, obviously homeless, directing the question at a young woman behind me. The woman was shrouded in a stylish raincoat (rain was in the forecast); in addition to the coat, she wore a plaid dress, black pumps, and a red beret— very European. She ignored the question and shifted her feet, nudging closer to me, now second in line. The man again asked, "Why are you dressed that way? You going somewhere?" Again the unpleasant smell entered my nostrils. Again the young woman moved a half step from him. She kept her glance focused in the distance. Her eyes, I noticed, were so clear that you might guess they belonged to a newborn.

She had a single piece of paper in her hand—was she seeking a library card? Then the same question entered my mind: why are you dressed so . . . becomingly? I would have guessed she toiled in an office—a mortgage company, a bank, a suite of rooms for public-interest lawyers. She certainly didn't belong to the university where, I had learned at a recent lecture, female professors now wore baggy pants and Birkenstock sandals. When they tried to dress nicely, they wore oversized Eileen Fisher sweaters.

"In New York people talk to me! You hear me?" The homeless man argued his case to himself, but no one else showed concern. He was a yawner, a sight seen again and again. Grumbling, he turned in a circle; to a clerk pushing a book cart, he said, "People talk to me in New York." But these people in the Berkeley Library were not ready for such antics so early in the morning. Coffee had yet to be drunk, pastries to be devoured, and fingers licked clean of sweetness. The poor guy, I noted, was clopping about in a pair of mismatched shoes.

THE FAILURE OF MEMORY

NOW WHERE WAS IT? In what book, what chapter and verse, the name of that noble in a small but bloody footnote in English history? I wake—a poet in need of a tale of bravery—wondering who the fellow was. We nail down the dates of importance—1066, for example. We read of lootings by Vikings, of castle sieges, of plagues that crawled up legs and pimpled faces with ghastly sores, of fires that leveled cities, of the

Globe and Lord Chamberlain's Men, the sordid stories of kings and queens, very few of whom we might call "huggable" in the present day—the stink of their unwashed bodies would bring tears to our eyes. If we are acquainted with the history of the English monarchy, we know of Charles I, who had his head severed. One observer among the mob on that day wrote, "There was such a Grone by the Thousands then present, as I never heard before & desire I may never hear again." That's a line for the ages.

I plow through my breakfast of cereal sugared with an overripe banana. I then check my bookshelf, my eyes moving left to right and up and down until they fall upon the word "English" along a spine. I pull Robert Lacey's *Great Tales from English History* off the shelf. I head to my chair in the corner of the living room, scan the table of contents, and start my quest on page 978, when Ethelred the Unready was wearing the crown. I recall that the half-remembered scene was at the end of a chapter, so I cruise the endings of chapters with headings like "Elmer the Flying Monk," "King Canute and the Thieves," and "A Prince of Thieves," with history, invariably bloody, raging on every page.

As the prose is lively, I pause to read some of the very short chapters—and would be happy to spend the entire day rediscovering Olde England—when I come upon the sought-after passage. The story involves Sir William Collingbourne during the rule of Richard III. The year is 1484. My interest? The treatment of *poet* William Collingbourne, who dared to pen a satiric rhyme directed at the king. He then further enraged the authorities by nailing it to the doors of St. Paul's Cathedral.

I've written poems lambasting politicians, celebrities, drunken priests, poets with literary trophies, out-of-print novelists, and in-print novelists—but none seemed to give a shit. Not one rose up in anger from a faux-leather recliner to retrieve a shotgun from the closet.

But Sir Collingbourne's taunt was considered treasonous. When he got wind that soldiers wished to speak to him, he rode away on a horse and hid in a village. But he was loud there too, drunkenly bragging in a tavern that he had written a little ditty about the king. He was discovered, jailed, spat at, ridiculed with hearty slaps, and so on. Then he was hauled back to London, where townies lined the streets and reveled in his public disgrace. A judge called for his execution. The poor fellow was strung up on the gallows (Aldergate, I wonder, or Execution Dock at Wapping?), brought down while his lungs were still heaving, castrated, and disemboweled.

But our Collingbourne was witty to the end. When the executioner shoved a hand into his abdomen and pulled out his slippery entrails, he said, "Oh, Lord Jesus, yet more trouble."

I touch my belly when I think of him, brave poet who spilled his guts for a poem.

PUBLIC DISPLAY OF AFFECTION

AFTER AN HOUR OF LEANING into younger men's bodies—we're speaking of pickup basketball here—I was a sweaty old man. I was wearing two layers of long-sleeved shirts, the better to force a lather of funk from my inner soul. Three straight games—half-court, three on three—had been sufficient. Exhausted, I benched myself. Fingers of sweat crawled down my face. A reservoir of stink darkened the front of my T-shirt. My breath, left behind somewhere, eventually returned.

I pushed off the bench and made my way to the drinking fountain by the baseball diamond. On the muddy trail to the watering hole, I spied a ponytailed girl reading my chapter novel, *Marisol*. She was seated comfortably on the grass, absorbed in a narrative in which the main character moves from Chicago's Pilsen neighborhood to the suburb of Des Plaines (at age ten, the same apparent age as this reader on the grass). Published in 2005, the novel came with a doll—some would reverse this order and say that the doll came with a book. In a very short period of time (one splendid November), the book became my best seller: 250,000 dolls went home with girls. Whether the novel was read or not, I didn't care because I, turncoat poet, received a sack of money that I swung first over my right shoulder and then over my left (it was a really heavy sack).

"Hi," I said, eager to admit that, yes, I wrote that book! What do you think of it? Do you have a question for me, author of the charming tale?

The girl gazed upward, using her finger as a bookmark. She was halfway through and, if memory served, Marisol, the girl hero, was searching for her cat, Rascal.

"You know," I continued, advancing the conversation, "I wrote that book." I smiled to give her evidence that, in spite of my sweaty appearance, I was an alright guy. When she returned an indifferent scowl, as if beholding a piece of irrelevant gum embedded in a sidewalk, I reeled in my smile. Nothing stirred in her, nothing moved her to even utter an, "Oh, really."

I hurried away to the water fountain and drank my fill in rapid gulps, afraid that the girl might skip off to her parents and report, "A dirty old man tried to talk to me." Then I headed home, without raising my eyes to the rearview mirror. This relationship was, like, over.

Later, I considered that the incident was not unlike a compact mirror, a piece of glass, a shattered taillight in the street—it reflected on my narrow experience. I had finally gotten my wish to see a reader, albeit a child reader, with a book of mine in hand. I had been awestruck by other authors—big shots like John Grisham and Stephen King—and the hefty sales that kept them living nicely. What was their reaction when they came upon a reader turning a page of one of their books? Perhaps, after that first elated encounter, the experience grows tiresome, a big yawner. Mr. Grisham *expects* readers, as does Mr. King. They expect their books to rise on the barometer of the best-seller list. Movies are made from the works of such authors; even when there are no movies, the heavy hitters yak it up, at least, on *Charlie Rose*. This is not my story, though. I've done the song and dance for producers and directors, and have even written to Oprah. Isn't it time, I begged, for a poet (slender and Hispanic, very appealing) to be crowned on her show?

The response from the global network? Silence.

I don't shirk my calling. I'm a poet with ink on my fingertips, with pencil lead on my tongue (licking the pencil revs it up). But the best I can look forward to is textbook publication, a title or two stocked in bookstores, and checks with three zeros at the end. I'm a poet among many, ranked somewhere near the top but not quite at the top. My literary pulse has slowed, but I'm happy to report that a magazine from the Midwest has taken two poems of mine.

And the ponytailed girl? She's now about sixteen, still a reader I pray, her passion for good stories begun on a warm afternoon many years ago, with the chapter novel *Marisol*, a one-time favorite until a dirty old man appeared, sweaty from leaning into young men.

WOOL CAP

IN THE EARLY 1980s my wife knitted me a wool cap with "Soto" embedded in its stitches. She worked on this cap for weeks, the needles clacking like the beaks of dueling ducks. Clack-clack, she worked by the fireplace. Clack-clack in the dining room and in front of the television.

The cap was the color of oatmeal. She gave it to me for Christmas. I wore it three times before losing it on a day when the sky was spitting pellets of icy rain. My wife didn't ask its whereabouts. She assumed that I was ungrateful, nothing new in that assumption, so true, so true. Carelessly I had lost my wool cap, so new that it was not yet scented with my hair. Then one day on the bus I saw a girl, age nine or ten, holding onto a pole as we rocked up Berkeley's University Avenue. She had bangs the color of oatmeal, cheeks the pink of "Be Mine" Valentine candy, and she was wearing my cap. I stood over her, a hand on the pole. With that cap on her, she couldn't have gotten any prettier. With it on me, I could have been a thief on my way to a burglary. I closed my eyes and saw my wife knitting her heart out for me, so true, so true. When I opened them, I saw my ungrateful face reflected in the window. "I like your cap," I told the girl. She raised her eyes; they were of the softest kind, not unlike a deer's. "Soto," she remarked, "is Spanish." Then she leveled her gaze and gripped the pole with both hands, as the brakes of the bus sighed. Inside, I sighed too. I had lost a very good gift.

Three stops later, I got off. The girl, so grateful, went on wearing what rightly belonged to her.

CITY LIGHTS

IN 1978, WHEN MY WIFE AND I first arrived in Berkeley, I occasionally drove to San Francisco, alone, to haunt City Lights, the bookstore. I recall descending the wooden stairs to the basement, the floorboards creaking like the knees of Beat poets, aged now, crazy now, spirited away now. I had teethed on their verse. I began reading Ginsberg in spring 1972 when I wanted to become a poet more than anything—more than money on the table, more than a regular job, more than marriage with a child in each window. The guru

Allen Ginsberg led me to Gregory Corso, Bob Kaufman, Lawrence Ferlinghetti, Michael McClure, Ed Dorn, and Kenneth Rexroth. I was confused then: could you cuss in poetry, or tell the country to fuck itself?

City Lights, founded not soon enough in 1953, is on Columbus and Broadway, with Chinatown on one side and the vanishing Italian neighborhood on the other. Three floors tall, it's unspectacular in architecture and situated near an alley where steam rises from street grates and old vegetables from Hunan-style restaurants ferment in buckled trash cans. This is what I hankered for, this urban scene, and that old-country Italian in a fedora weaving home up Columbus. Poorly played accordion music wafted from an open window, and the sounds of pots and pans promised a sumptuous meal.

On our arrival from Fresno, I had to see this fabled corner, to enter this temple where books scaled the walls from floor to ceiling. And this I did, many times, and in a leather jacket too—so poetic. The small-press literary magazines and books were housed in the basement, a treasure trove of current publications. There, I thumbed pages, read at length, recognized names, wrote down addresses, and dreamed until I levitated with ambition. With each magazine, I thought: I want to be in this one . . . and this one . . . and this one. I had already published one book of poems, *The Elements of San Joaquin*, and another was on its way. I had published in the *Iowa Review*, the *North American Review*, and the *New Yorker*, well-known magazines that, to my astonishment, paid in real currency. But I hankered to see my name in a plethora of small-press magazines, ones that would be around for three or four issues, then fold, like laundry. I imagined other poets seeing my name repeatedly, that upstart Gary Soto—not Gary Snyder, but Gary Soto—winner of one award and with others, like cargo from Asia, heading this way and soon!

There were chapbooks too, small stapled jobs but also fine-press ones. I craved being part of this world. My ambition included a smartly done chapbook of a work-in-progress, which I would hand out to friends and enemies alike. (Eventually a publisher did bring out a chapbook of my poetry. One evening at a Cody's Books reading, in 1982, I tried my best to peddle this twelve-page folio for fifty cents—I sold two.)

The City Lights poetry section was located in an alcove, behind a freestanding bookshelf, hidden away, as if it were porno. I summoned up *kayak*, a sloppily printed magazine (their trademark) which included the likes of Hayden Carruth, W. S. Merwin, Charles Simic, John Haines, Morton Marcus, and Robert Mezey. I sent poems regularly to this magazine, and George Hitchcock, the editor, returned them regularly, with a slash of his signature and the note, "Thanks but no."

I pondered the blue ink from George Hitchcock's pen—the note was a tribute, I figured, because his truly thoughtful response included "thanks." For me, this implied that, within my poetry, there was something to be thankful for, and I had to remain positive in spite of rejection.

Occasionally a visitor would sidle up to the alcove. I would gaze up, take him in, and see that often he, too, wore a leather jacket. If it was a female visitor, eyes bruised from lack of sleep, she would be shrouded in a navy peacoat, the perfume of cigarettes embedded in the woolly fabric. I recall one visitor—a stink was about him—who thumbed through the pages of a chapbook that I had held a minute before. He treated it recklessly, actually licking his finger to turn the page—his spit on the edge of a fine-press chapbook! He also bent the book so that it cracked—a chiropractor relieving the pain of verse.

I recall another visitor sighing. What was he reading that touched him? A poem of death, heartache, forced employment because of marriage? I waited for him to leave. When he did, I took his place and opened up *Poetry Now*, a tabloid newsprint. I read some of the poems but didn't feel any sighs building up within me. They were good but not brilliant, nothing worth sighing about.

On these visits to City Lights, I seldom bought a magazine or book. I was poor then, with just a few dollars in my wallet. At the night's end, I headed to Vesuvio, the bar next to the bookstore, where I splurged on a single beer, bitter medicine to put me in the mood. Careful not to spill my precious brew, I wound my way up a staircase to a cramped space with tables and chairs. From this vantage point I looked out at the strip joint where Carol Doda, the biggest girl in town, danced on a platform above sad customers with watery beers.

I sipped like a bird, and sipped again. I was in a special place—twenty-six years old, with long black locks and a leather jacket. On the second floor of Vesuvio, I sat where the Beats sat, their cigarette smoke curling into the shapes of question marks—what is the meaning of life? I was born too late to join their ranks, now nearly depleted, but I became a poet because of them, and I acknowledge them. I sat alone, with a poem taken from my back pocket. I revised on the beer-sticky tabletops to keep myself looking busy. How I raised my head, how my heart kicked up a little dance when I heard footsteps pound up the staircase. Was this Ginsberg coming? Kaufman? Corso with his shirt-tail hanging out? I expected these legends to appear, weary from writing into the morning, weary of the police and crummy politicians, weary of admirers such as me.

If they wanted drinks, I wouldn't have hesitated to use my last dollar.

HERE'S WHAT I THINK

I OPEN A FILE WHERE THE CORPSES of dead poems are kept, poems that never saw publication, dozens so poorly rendered that I wince. Were my creative faculties on strike when I put pen to paper? Was I hungover? Was I starving for nourishment other than the wood of a bitten pencil? I have distanced myself from these sorry efforts, yet I come clean and provide a few titles: "Local History Lesson," "No Frills," "Christian Self-Doubt," "A Friend Sells Advice," "Come Back, Dog," "The Blue Cavalry and the Tripped-Up Indians," "A Summer's End." I quote the beginning lines of the last one:

> The last well-fed flies rolled onto their backs,
> Buzzed once, and died in sunlight. It was autumn.
> Apples dropped from trees, their cores
> Centered with the question marks of worms . . .

The poem spurts along with adequate imagery and ends quizzically with:

> When the water of knowledge flowed beneath me,
> I drank through my mad and tangled roots.

Huh? The poem was unceremoniously buried ten years ago but recently exhumed—my brow furrows from its putridity. Any poet who has been writing for decades has such poems filed away. But for every blooper, we poets might get two or three keepers—this is my ration, at least: one bad one, two or three worth their weight in ink.

How do I get my poems done? By striking two sticks together? Yanking on the braids of the barmaid muse? Plucking at a tuned lyre? I have my routine: read poetry in the morning and remember that a poem is a canvas—for God's sake, I tell myself, be a Dutch painter, be Van Eyck. I follow this dictum: strong, not weak, specification. After all, readers hanker for fresh language, not the overused, tired language served daily in our print world. In short, I argue for surprising language coupled with a surprising narrative or lyric. To quote John Updike: "An expected kiss is not worth giving."

No elaboration, no discourse. My approach could be picked apart savagely by other poet/critics. I have poet friends who teach—or would like to teach—who are prepared to offer elegant defenses when critiquing student writing. If not done carefully, even gingerly, the student poets growl in their hearts, "You're stupid." Or an irate and injured student may skip the heart and just snarl and rant, then report that part-timer to the ombudsman. Anemic part-timers, already paid poorly, why must they suffer more? I recall when I *did* teach and was one day busily critiquing a poem, a hand went up from the back row. I stopped and asked,

"Yes, a question?" The young woman asked, "Are you a wetback?"

Oh, Jesus and his unarmed apostles! Was she listening to any kernel of wisdom to ferry away?

Because I write for children and young adults, teachers assume that I would like to talk about the writing process, especially to answer the inevitable question, "Where do you get your ideas?" Oh, please, let's not do this, I beg. That I get my work done is all that I care about; rumination on such a mundane topic spoils my day.

But I recall a poet who uttered, "Listen to your inner voice," to a wagon train of school chairs filled with bright-looking teens. We were in the Midwest at a college no one has ever heard of; I believe it was spring, with nice puffy clouds heading east. My colleague was truly tenderhearted, sensitive, and properly educated. Words flew from her bud-shaped mouth like blossoms. My own mouth hung open like a potato sack. I was enthralled with how she parried any bad feelings as she lovingly critiqued a bad line—dang, I could learn from her, I thought. I remembered her tactics when I was asked to visit Fresno Juvenile Hall. I was led by invisible chains to face thirteen kids in orange suits that matched the plastic chairs they filled. The burly director said that these incarcerated young people were writing poetry. He introduced me by saying that

I was one of them—*raza*. I could see that one *vato* was well-advanced in his creative journey. Across his forehead a large tattoo, in two-inch letters at least, proclaimed: "Fresno." I wanted to ask, "Hey, where you from?" but bit my tongue.

I smiled. I remembered the poet whose mouth was bud-like. As much as physically possible, I shaped mine into a tidy bud and imagined blossoms perfuming the overlit room. But I didn't have it in me to convince my audience that what they were hearing wasn't bad stuff. I read a poem, and then another poem, one after another, with a swamp in my armpits. I could see the reception when I finally looked up from my book. Their heads hung like the guilty, hands folded in prayer that this sucker might end and they could return to their bunks. I tried the line, "Listen to your inner voice." This prompted one budding Pinto poet to say, "This is hella boring—I got to take a shit."

You see, I don't possess the power to teach others of the artistry in writing poetry. I just have my own routine. For me: read other poets and remember to be a Dutch painter—the canvas must be filled with clear imagery through strong specification.

Let's just leave it at that.

PIGEONS

THERE WOULD BE NO HANDOUT for the unfor-
tunate brother on Shattuck Avenue. "Sir, sir," he
said, "I know we're different colors, but may I talk
to you?" I kept my attention focused ahead, aware of
his red-eyed presence on my left. I lowered my gaze
to the pavement and the rain rinsing it clean. I passed
the man, heavyhearted, and flinched when he said,
mournfully, "I thought your color was a good color."
I should have turned then, with my hand searching a
front pocket. But I failed there, and my heart buckled,
as if it were made of tin. I could have given him a dollar and reflected, not unlike the light on the wet street,
on his meaning: "I thought your color was a good
color." It was a piece of poetry, a line uttered and lost
on a rainy day. Was brown a better color than black?

At the corner loitered two pigeons, little scam artists,
their eyes like miniature targets. Were they stoned?
Had they picked up a roach and inhaled a couple of
puffs? If they could have spoken, they might have said,
"I know we have feathers and you have hair and skin,
but can we talk?" If they had said that, I would have
bought them burgers, with the works.

DOWNSIZING

MY WIFE HAS GOTTEN RID OF BOLTS of fabric, yards of it, enough to cut and stitch sails for a millionaire's yacht. She has tossed burnt light bulbs—maracas if you shake them—and, from a bulletin board, she has unpinned clothing designs, some of which were her own pencil work, others snipped from magazines. She has stuffed bags with sundries, which I will ferry to the Creative Reuse in Oakland, a Santa Claus hoisting goodies over my shoulder.

Now in our sixties, we consider downsizing. I patrol the garage, former home to our Saturn, the discontinued dinosaur. But what are we to do with two hammers, three flashlights, the tool kit that came with the Saturn, the opera binoculars (when were they bought?), the deflated basketball, only a single sigh remaining inside its synthetic skin. The flower vases—thirteen, like the apostles—I'll place them in a box and call the box an ark. They're sailing away too.

In the rafters are paint cans, artwork bought and forgotten, baby clothes that outfitted our daughter, a lamp shade like a ballroom gown, college textbooks, kitchen tiles, a lost shuttlecock, and a network of conspiring spiders. I peek at the side of the house, where stand weeds like spears and, among the weeds, a hoe and a rusty shovel. I'll break them in halves and fit them into the garbage can. A work glove with a digit pointing skyward—that goes in the garbage as well.

I return inside and browse the bookshelves. Sorry, Anita Brookner, ambassador of fine prose but repeated chronicler of spinsters surviving on squeezed tea bags. You'll have to find a new home, like Lorrie Moore, Hilary Mantel, P. G. Wodehouse, John Galsworthy, John Updike, Walter Mosley, W. S. Merwin, and grandfatherly Robert Frost, who took the right path and got all the prizes. Then I hesitate: there is *New and Selected Poems* by my late friend Leonard Nathan, birder, translator, and poet unashamed of the ascot that hugged his throat and which was itself a colorful, exotic bird. I take the book off the shelf and turn it over. His photo on the back cover pleads, "Don't do it, Gary."

My collection of poetry is a columbarium, each book in its tidy place and no visitors for months, if not years.

LISTS

IN 1999, MY BOOK *Living Up the Street* was included in the *San Francisco Chronicle's* Western 100. Indeed, it was ranked numero sixty-five—between *The Legacy of Conquest: The Unbroken Past of the American West*, by Patricia Nelson Limerick, and *The Captive Mind*, by Czesław Miłosz, winner of a Nobel Prize in literature. I own a copy of the latter book, which contains some heady essays, but not the former. I may search for a copy of Limerick's book in the library, just to see. As for finding it in bookstores—forget it! Books that don't move are like cartons of milk, taken off the shelf one day after they expire. What happens to milk? Down a gullet called the drain. What happens to books? The indifferent teeth of giant shredders.

Readers might be surprised to learn that books, like love, are not forever. But this is part of nature to poets and writers, all loveless when we go out of print. We publish a book and pray it sprints into the arms of readers. Read us, we beg, please read us!

How did *Living Up the Street* find its skinny spine on this bulwark of commendable titles? And why that position? Why wasn't it number twelve or eighty-seven? Number one belongs to Mary Austin's *Land of Little Rain*, one hundred to *Anybody's Gold*, by Joseph Henry Jackson. (In 1985, I was runner-up for a Bay Area fellowship named after Jackson.)

Many of these books are familiar to me: I note Edward Abbey's *Desert Solitaire* positioned at number three, Joan Didion's *The White Album* at nine, Hong Kingston's *The Woman Warrior* at forty-two, Thompson's *Fear and Loathing* at forty-six, Wolff's *This Boy's Life* at fifty. I pause when it occurs to me that Didion's *Slouching Towards Bethlehem* is not among the top finishers. How is this possible? That book for me—for thousands in search of California—was so helpful in illuminating the 1960s. That this book was not included is not worrisome, however. It is not tragic. Didion might have driven all the way to the bank, crying. But, in the parking lot, she would've dabbed her mascara before going in with her loot.

Then there is *The Hispanic 100*, compiled by Himilce Novas and published in 1995. Here, I'm positioned at sixty-seven. There's a three-page account of my life story, which a reader doing research could easily feed into his/her homework. (This was before Wikipedia.) But why am I ranked between tennis sensation Pancho Segura and golf legend Chi Chi Rodriguez? I have to swallow my embarrassment and kick a stone—because the ranking is unjust. Pancho, I know tennis. You deserve a higher position. And Chi Chi, you're the man—*el mero mero*—among Mexican American golfers.

The number-one Hispanic of all time is Cesar Chavez, labor leader. There's no quibble here, no grumblings.

But how is Henry Cisneros, disgraced politician (and presently a businessman), positioned just behind tenor Placido Domingo? What did Cisneros do besides go to meetings? Or why is Father Junípero Serra number four? What would American Indians think of this? Serra was not above using a whip to get them to build missions up and down California. I think of an Indian in Baja who lamented, at the arrival of Christianity, "O, please, take your God away." Why are there only six writers? Two classical singers? Two serious musicians—wait a minute, isn't Pablo Casals a European, not an American? And what about Luis Alvarez, a scientist with a brain the size of a huge cauliflower? I never saw the *vato* in *el barrio*. Maybe he was too smart to hang with *raza*.

This list has a reference book feel to it. It's hefty, incomplete, and on a library shelf seldom visited. Because so much has occurred since the mid-1990s, the compiler could easily shuffle some names and add others. J-Lo would have to be added, for instance, and Ricky Martin, after he came out of that really swanky closet. If a new version is brought out, my position will have sunk, I'm sure, or disappeared entirely, ranked 101 and sliding down.

A DOG STORY

FOR YEARS I BELIEVED DOGS were faithful and that, by extending a paw, they portioned out kindness to lonely men. We were, after all, the ones who opened cans that scented the air with processed meat by-products. We also cleaned their bowls of paddling flies and playfully chimed the tags under their chins. We ferried them to vets. We walked them around the block and back again. We hugged them and pulled their snouts toward our necks. We petted them and cooed, "Good boy!"

One afternoon, after yet another rejection from a small literary magazine in the Midwest, I was in need of a dog's affection. A cockapoo suddenly appeared. My heart raced! I called to him with a singsong whistle. I clicked my fingers at this highbred pooch in the park. He, dressed in an ascot, quivered his snout at my attempt at friendship. How dare I snap my fingers at him, his posture insinuated. He raised his mug nobly, a few inches into the air, sniffed at my unpleasantness, and wheeled away. The dog dissed me! He held his tail high, revealing a leaf attached to his anus. Had his owner trained him to wipe? Had the dog evolved that far? Would he be on the toilet next, reading the *Wall Street Journal*?

If he were a Fresno dog, low on self-esteem, high on street smarts, he would summon from memory my kind hand. He would recall the cold rain that I stroked from his fur with a dish towel, and remember how my fingers patrolled his fur for fleas. That bone with gristle, he couldn't forget. But this cockapoo with the ascot! He didn't even peek over his shoulder. Instead, as a last insult, he scraped his hind feet on the ground, as if sweeping dirt on a steaming turd.

I had left the house to burn away my moodiness in sunlight. I had received more rejection letters; they came regularly, and from magazines that used to favor my work. But I was too weak to allow myself to be offended, either by rejection or this high-and-mighty asshole dog. I walked around, hands in my pockets, until the wind tipped my hat forward. For a few seconds, I was blinded. Then I tapped my hat back onto my head. The leaves were going one way, and I the other—so contrary, as my wife says, so uncooperative am I. If I were a goose, she tells me, I would fly north when my chum birds were winging south.

True.

I returned home, resolving to rip up five rejection letters (a month's haul) in one bout of anger. I tore through the layers of bad news, completing the task without my hearing aid tumbling out of my ear. I made confetti of those rejection letters, put on my coat, went back outside, and crossed into the park, where I showered the letters onto Lake Merritt. Geese sped over and began to peck at the debris, swallowing everything, words like, "thanks," "sorry," "next time," and, most painful of all, "Dear Larry."

What I really need is a dog.

M&MS

HOW MUCH MEMORY IS ENOUGH? How much can a writer siphon from the gorged heart of experience and yet have the heart still pump? If one cares about the mystery of childhood, as a good many poets do, then the well is amazingly deep. The subjects rebound, sometimes effortlessly and sometimes with the stubbornness of a frog that won't leap. I'm thinking of my flickering life, age four, and me standing late at night on the back porch where my brother and I slept. I'm eating M&Ms, examining each one by the glow of the streetlight at the corner of Van Ness and Braly avenues. I'm searching for the red ones, tastier than the green, yellow, and orange ones—even better than the brown ones.

This was one of my first memories, me with my hoard of M&Ms. I was protective of them, greedy.

My brother was in his cot, asleep: good news for me. I had no plans to share. This was my life, and this was me, age four, partially lit by a light on a street that I had yet to cross alone.

MY TIME WITH JOHN MALKOVICH'S ASSISTANT

IN 1997 I RECEIVED A CALL from Shannon Clark of Mr. Mudd, a film company in Southern California. Their new film, *Ghost World*, had just been released to fabulous reviews and other works were scheduled, including *Juno*. Ms. Clark asked if my young adult novel *Buried Onions* was available. I turned to the shelf where I kept my stash—that title as well as other novels, essays, and poetry collections. I gulped. Here was my chance to enter the big leagues, I thought. Don't blow it! No film company, large or small, known or unknown, rich or broke, had ever called to inquire about my books, "properties" as they say in the industry.

Mr. Mudd is owned by three savvy veterans of theater, among them John Malkovich, an artist's artist. The company was taken by my novel, which had appeared three years earlier and still had legs, though thin ones. School districts were buying this book in bulk. Students were writing me and saying, in poor penmanship, "I like how the dude gets killed."

A few weeks later, I flew to Bob Hope Airport in Burbank, rented an economy car, and found Mr. Mudd's office, which was located in an old building, fashionably hip, in a trendy area of Los Angeles. Having arrived early, I had an hour to whittle from my life. Thus, on foot, I scouted the surrounding residential neighborhood, which was leafy and tidy, with sprinklers raining on fertilized lawns. Wind chimes hung from eaves, and exotic cars sat in driveways. I could see myself living among these citizens, provided there was a pool to dip a toe in after a day of writing scripts—fuck poetry. I imagined a thick, white bathrobe with my sleeves monogrammed GS.

With the hour used up, I made my appearance at the office. I met Ms. Clark, then two of the three principal owners of the company. They listened to me as I pounded out my story; at one junction, I proclaimed that every Fresno grape had my sweaty tears inside them. I had no idea what I meant by that, and they didn't either. They pretended not to hear. I was excited by meeting people who knew people. What was I but a dog wagging my tail?

"Lunch," the producer announced. "How does that sound?"

Lunch at a restaurant called One, walking distance—why not? It seemed like the entire staff was invited—nine of us in caterpillar fashion going through the door—the highlight of the day for many of them. The table was long as a limo. I sat near the middle, my glee now softened. What I was required to fit in was a pair of sunglasses on top of my head. Already I was becoming jaded. I was going to splurge and have the saddles at my waists sculpted by liposuction.

I ordered an exotic-sounding sandwich from a diploma-sized paper menu. The sandwich came with a cold soup and potato salad. I ordered an Italian soda, as alcohol during lunch makes me talk like a fool. I looked around the table for the cue to eat. I ate when Ms. Clark began her soup. I was happy to be somewhere new in my life. I recall that the crowd was young, all with cell phones before there were really cell phones. They were going places.

I enjoyed the presence of these young people who were not mapped out with tattoos that began at their necks and scrolled down to God-knows-what parts of their shaved and unshaved bodies. This was a clean group. I liked them all, and I liked where I was. In my mind, my pool had expanded, with a diving board for the mermaid starlets and a slide for the kiddy actors who would play roles based on my children's books.

Were these my thoughts? Yes, I admit them, silly as they are, and I admit that my eyes floated regularly to one blonde lassie on the end. I couldn't help myself. My sandwich, with its layer of sprouts, was engaging but not that engaging. With a fork, I explored the potato salad, but this starchy side dish also held little interest for me. I tried to keep my eyes on my meal or the executive producer to my left but, like former President Carter, there was lust in my heart.

In the film world, you don't imbibe tap water from God-knows-what source—a canal from my hometown, Fresno? Let's not do that! No, this crowd had Italian fizzy water and, after lunch, coffees in cups little larger than thimbles. Some of the young people departed with cell phones stationed at their ears. They had to go to work, but others lingered. I got up and went to the head, to release some of the Italian water drunk at a restaurant called One—how cool was that?

"This is it, Gary," I said to the mirror. I checked my teeth and rinsed my hands in hot water, as if they were cutlery. I closed my eyes: the blonde assistant appeared, clacking a pencil between her top and bottom teeth. Just what was her job?

On my return, the blonde assistant gazed up—so flirty! Perhaps she considered me someone in the making. She did me the favor of spreading her legs, just slightly, so that I could take a sneak preview—the white panties like a surrender flag. I was in my mid-forties, and I was a man like any other, provided you liked women. If I had been wearing a toupee, it would have flown off my head. The view of panties was pleasant. I wondered: are they wet?

Thank you, I thought in my heart. Thank you, thank you.

I bid farewell to the producers and returned home nibbling Southwest peanuts. This was the first step, the initial meeting. By all appearances, *Buried Onions* would get a green light.

Over the next year, a script was written, actors lined up, a director brought in from Mexico City. A CD presenting Fresno and Fresno's gang life was made. The music was loud, like someone standing inches from you and yelling, "Bitch."

But then two years passed, and two more years. I approached my fifties, then entered my fifties. The calls from Ms. Clark became less frequent, but my heart leapt when I learned that they had re-titled the project *Hystoria*.

Two more years after that, my options—a couple thousand dollars a year—stopped.

The film project became history. My novel with the tiring legs—the property—sank into a pool I never owned. And the blonde assistant? Gone for all I know.

MY MFA ARRIVES BY MAIL

IT WAS PAST NOON, a good part of the day torn off like a chunk of bread. Earlier I had received my MFA diploma by mail and used the tube it came in first as a telescope (job prospects are very small when you squint), then a trumpet ("Jon," I called to a friend with his own MFA that year, "what are you doing?"), and finally a gavel on the side of my head. In short, I was bored. My wife was off at work in an air-conditioned office and I was alone, tired of poetry and the buzz of a fly—was that you, Emily Dickinson?

I left our apartment in a clean T-shirt, the light as bright as a scalpel. I had to find a job, something like the city workers hosing off the sidewalk. I can do that, I told myself as I walked past the duo in orange vests. One hosed while his amigo ate a spotted banana, watching the water flow. Afterward they would get into the truck and head off to another place, where the one eating the banana would hose and the other would eat or drink. A sweaty brew was beginning to surface on my brow.

> The sun is coin bright.
> The busted condom is a wayward child twelve
> years from the day.
> The sea peels back the beach.

The poetry inside me was really bad, all because of the arc of sun, which had dazed me. On a bank sign, the temperature read 104 degrees. Darkness showed under my arms. What path had I taken during midday? The one where I sweat and people in air-conditioned cars think, "What's that stupid guy doing?"

After a half-mile this way, a half-mile that way, I returned home, my ambitions depleted from the heat. I drank water and, like William Carlos Williams, went to the refrigerator for a plum. I then lay shirtless on the bed, a tall glass of water with ice cubes within arm's reach. I read a poem by Mark Strand—didn't believe the sentiment. I read a poem by Edward Field—now here was a real poet. But I soon grew drowsy. There was no ocean breeze to pour into our apartment. The fumes of sadness circled in the wind of a two-speed fan. I fell asleep, mouth open, and dreamed nothing. I woke to my wife chirping, "Gary, where are you? It's hot in here. Poor baby."

I woke limp as old celery (more bad poetry), sat on the edge of the bed. I was tired but I hadn't done anything except walk a few blocks and read poetry in the breeze of our fan. Wake up! I scolded myself. Get it together!

"Carolyn," I called hoarsely, desperate for another person, for no one had spoken to me except poems. I yawned and was grateful for the springs inside the mattress when I pushed off. I went to the living room and hugged her first from the front and then from the back.

"Gary," she asked after I released her. "What did you do today?"

"Nothing," I answered proudly, for a poet to get a real job means the end. I led her by the hand to the kitchen table. I showed her my diploma and the mailing tube it came in. She hugged me some more and asked if she could have the tube.

That evening, Carolyn went off to see friends. Once again alone, except for some hoodlum voices in poetry I read after a dinner of two sandwiches, I took a bowl of Jell-O to the yard. There I sat under a sycamore, its dusty leaves hiding long abandoned nests. The summer heat had sucked me of poetry, crushed my spirit to mow the lawn, and put anger in my eyes—why was I born in Fresno and not Alaska or Ireland? Then, as I slurped a first spoonful of Jell-O, I imagined Patagonia and penguins applauding the arrival of icebergs on a shore.

I sat in a webbed lawn chair, shirtless. I glowered at my mountainous Jell-O, medicine for tonsil patients and teething babies. But I was neither. I was a young man slick as a human-sized tuna. It was still hot, and sweat was what I would do. I looked skyward: the godless stars were chewing what I could only believe were ice cubes. The heavens were cold, or at least cool.

When the phone rang, I hurried inside to answer it and hear a friend ask, "Did you get yours?" It was Jon Veinberg, newly minted MFA student, class of 1976. He was speaking of our diplomas.

"Yeah," I answered. Jon and I spent our graduate school years drinking and listening to rock and roll. "Are you going to have yours framed?"

"Hell no!" Jon blasted.

After the call I returned outside. I stared at my bowl of Jell-O, now syrupy as blood. I breathed in and breathed out. I thought of my wife: she was somewhere in Fresno with girlfriends. She was in an air-conditioned house, I knew, and she was maybe eating Jell-O that was whole and cold and a color other than blood.

My diploma went into a binder and the tube went to a cool place.

LIKABLE

THERE'S AN INSECT FROM BELIZE that can eject its brain and still crawl several days before it stops, on a leaf perhaps, frozen in midchew. I will admit to such vacancy between my own ears. Last week I joined my wife and friends at a jazz festival in Fresno's Chinatown, threw back a bucket of beer, and nibbled nothing but French fries and California rolls. I sat in a chair, nodding my head to the thump of the stand-up bass. When the booze took hold, I became sullen, not unlike a toad, with my toad mouth pulled down. I was drunk, and I was a toad. My wife, disgusted, drove to our country abode in West Fresno, while I leaned my head on the window. She showed me the bed and ordered, "Go to sleep."

Spin time, with closets of dirty things spinning behind my eyelids. It was ugly. And yet, in this Laundromat of a spin cycle, I argued, *My wife loves me, I know she does*, though she had moved without my knowing to the couch. Later, I staggered outside to yak on a rosebush. The yuck splattered on the bush and on the garden hose. In the moon's glare, I looked down: so that's what California rolls look like when they've been inside a stomach for a while.

I woke with a pulsating hurt inside my head and guided myself into the living room by touching the walls. My wife loves me, she will always love me. I blinked at her on our yellow couch. I swallowed. I attempted to form words of morning greetings, but I had ejected my brain, like that insect in Belize. My mouth was dry, and my arms surprisingly power- less—alcohol will do that. But I figured that a new brain would, like a cauliflower, grow back in a day. My wife—how adorable—was reading an old issue of *Better Homes and Gardens*. She didn't look up when she turned the page. In a flat voice, she said, "There's a sturdy dog outside eating your vomit."

Marriage is good, marriage is bad. I'm alive, and Dylan Thomas and drunks like him are dead, all sucked by roots and shit. These were some of my thoughts as I went out onto the cement porch and, yes, there was man's best friend, thick in coat and red in both eyes, sitting by the first row of the vineyard. He raised his large head, tongue like a small necktie. He licked his chops. I had a sudden thought: After a night of drinking, there *is* still something likable inside me. Why else would this sturdy dog be whipping his tail about, on his feet in anticipation of another flowering of yuck?

BOOK TITLES

THE LONGEST BOOK TITLE IN LITERARY HISTORY? It may belong to Sir Walter Raleigh, author of *The Discovery of the Large, Rich, and Beautiful Empire of Guiana, with a Relation of the Great and Golden City of Manoa, Which the Spaniards Called El Dorado, and the Provinces of Emeria, Aromaia, Amapaia, and Other Countries, with Their Rivers Adjoining*. The book was written in 1596 or so, while Raleigh was in the West Indies, and not in the Tower of London where he was jailed on charges of treason against King James—the years were 1612–1616, I believe. There he married Elizabeth Throckmorton, one of Queen Elizabeth's maids of honor. There he fathered a son he named Carew. There he wrote *The History of the World*, a much tidier book title, composed with a quill dipped into ink. Outside the Thames River must have looked like ink, dark and thick, full of histories untold, and with humans rocking between waves and slowly pushing out to sea. On the river, ducks clacked their beaks like swords and poked each other's eyes. A squealing pig might have slipped out of its owner's arms to take its chances on the river—anything but a long knife run up its belly? The pig would have drowned and floated away with its trotters set straight in the air.

In Raleigh's late winters, the sky must have boiled with ink-colored clouds and dyed the miserable townies with something like ash.

TRANSLATIONS

I RECEIVED A LETTER from Michael Matto, a former student of mine when I taught at Cal Berkeley, and now professor at Adelphi University in Garden City, New York. The letter, as formal and crisp as its stationery, invited me to translate Anglo-Saxon poetry for a book project. Rough translations would be provided. Anglo-Saxon poetry, I thought, envisioning Vikings rowing up the Thames, AD 980. Around the campfire, the Vikings employed their enemy's arrows as toothpicks, using them to unhinge gristly meat from their molars.

I envisioned slaughtered townies, fire crawling up wooden churches, plunder in the hulls of long ships, and the Picts, an ancient people, hiding in forests, so afraid to come out that they became extinct. The Picts would leave only bronze bracelets, shards of earthenware, and their bones. The Picts were not big people; they weren't brave; they disappeared.

I was easily recruited for the project and couldn't wait to get started. In the end I translated riddles, a form of poetry often associated with primitive people. They were enjoyable to render into contemporary English. I did one after another but only a handful were chosen—I couldn't hog the anthology. Here are two from that final collection.

"The Wind Sends Small Creatures"
The wind sends small creatures
From the other side of the headlands:
Feathery as grain, fine as smoke,
They arrive dark but brighten to chirm and clamor.
They are many, an army to themselves,
Angling for the green pond but not touching down.
We folks know them from a distance,
Salute them with hands over our furrowed brows.
As they toot the language of trees,
We recognize a common song.

(starlings)

"At Rest, Laborers Lean on Me"
At rest, laborers lean on me,
Then lead me to the barn
To pitch feed at drooling cattle.
I'm both tooth and nose,
A hurtful thing if you're a barking dog.
I herd chicken droppings to the fence,
Scratch the garden's terraced rows,
And drag the fields for an early summer harvest.
On my prongs, I lift wheat into a golden pile.
A hero to the laborer,
I return home riding on his shoulder!
If you look closely, you'll see smeared bee and moth,
Maybe an errant flower,
Just past blooming.

(a rake)

I have also translated one Pablo Neruda poem for Ilan Stavans's *The Poetry of Pablo Neruda*. Otherwise I have stayed away from translating, for I possess only talent enough to bungle my own poems and not the works of others.

POOCH, WHO ARE YOU NAMED FOR?

I FLEW INTO ATLANTA, took a bus to my hotel, checked in, and walked the streets where Dr. Martin Luther King Jr. lived and preached. I walked past historic Fire Station No. 6, The King Center, his childhood home, the Ebenezer Baptist Church, his stately tomb adorned with wreaths and flowers. I was wilting from the heat, which was like a subway ride in August. I was glad to be there, though. I walked Auburn Street, me, a natural man, a grown and curious man, a sigh building up inside me—if only Dr. Martin Luther King Jr. had lived.

Why was I in the Deep South? I had been invited to address an elementary school teachers' conference. I saw swarms of teachers in the streets, wearing lanyards that named their school districts. I saw them in bars, all of them happy and making the best of their time. The next morning I did a breakout session with about forty teachers and university types, many from surrounding suburbs. I was clear-eyed, very clever. In twenty minutes I argued that ethnic literature should be written by ethnic writers, that syrupy stories about Mexican farm laborers were written only by fake-ass opportunistic white children's writers who should get a life. In short, I put the nails in my own newly sawed coffin. A few in the audience walked out. I bit a knuckle from disgust with myself.

After my rant I was led to the exhibit hall where I sat behind a table with a dull maroon skirt. It was time for my book signing. A steady line of book buyers put me in a better mood. Then the line petered out. I wagged my pen, like a tail, and waited, not in the least jealous of the author at the adjoining table, who had admirers all over her. Suddenly a large woman approached, towing a small cart, the kind that hauls produce from a market. I hoisted a smile. She ran a chubby hand across her brow and said, towering above me, "I hope I didn't bring too many." She began to lift books from the cart. The stack grew like a pyramid; I recognized some of the books as out of print.

"Not at all," I answered, the pen uncapped and ready to go. "Who should I dedicate them to?" To her class, she told me—no, to the school library, if I didn't mind. As no others were waiting in line, I did what I was told. She was a lovely woman, a dedicated reader. I considered her a friend—no, more than a friend. She told me that she liked my books so much that she named her dog "Soto." My pen stopped. I looked up. It was like receiving word that I had been awarded the Nobel Prize. I wanted to hug the woman who delivered such joyful news. "What kind of dog is it?" I asked. She smiled, her arms full of my dog-eared books. "Why," she said, "a Chihuahua, of course."

FULL ATTENTION

A 1967 PHOTO SHOWS CESAR CHAVEZ in England. He is speaking to two labor unionists, explaining his efforts to bring better pay and better working conditions to farm workers. The photo is black-and-white and the best example I've ever encountered of full attention. The body language of the two unionists tells me they are in disbelief—not of Chavez himself but of the information that he is conveying about the agricultural strikes in the 1960s. The conversation among the three men is in an early stage, I would guess. Perhaps Chavez has been introduced just minutes before, because the unionists are not expressing disgust, anger, or a what-the-fuck attitude. But their eyes are on him—and the processing will occur very soon. It is a moment the men will not forget.

Reading poetry is likewise an act of attention. You use the imagination you've been given to conjure a scene, stir it around, and do your best to understand its meaning—or at least gauge its level of feeling. To do less suggests laziness. I recall reading W. S. Merwin's poetry, particularly *The Carrier of Ladders,* not grasping it all but giving my attention fully. Merwin was a master poet as well as a translator of numerous languages. He had to know something!

His poetry then, as now, has a mystical feel, and its ambiguity is worth quartering like an apple.

What the heck is inside?

Seeds from others poems studied when he was a
young man.

AFTER READING SIX PAGES FROM THE NEW TESTAMENT

I HAVE CHOSEN TO LIVE TO 120, just like Moses,
who sustained himself on manna. With all this time,
I'll write poems, send them to magazines in the
Midwest, have them accepted, have them rejected,
and have them misfiled and lost. A long life is what I
want, tenure in this greenish university we call Earth.
Will I look like shit at that age, a reptile hugging an
Amazonian tree trunk? I open the New Testament: the
prophets are preaching by calm waters; saints are pulling miracles from their long, dirty sleeves. I should
check out an audiotape of this ancient book from the
library, even though my daughter, a veterinarian with
plenty of knowledge upstairs, tells me I'm no scholar.

To hear that I'm no scholar is about the best thing
that has entered and exited my ears. I opt for life. As
an old salt, I'll smoke a corncob pipe on a wharf where
seagulls bicker over dropped bait. As a poet with a
feminine side, I'll collect saltshakers with corked
bottoms. As a retired professor with health benefits,

I'll volunteer several hours a week at a food bank. Exhausted, I'll come home and climb into my recliner, nod off like a cadaver, stiff in the joints, the hinge of my jaw hanging open.

I can't remember today's breakfast, but I can recall my youth—when I spoon-fed a sick dog. The dog didn't live more than five hours after I administered my prescription. But the spoon, washed and shiny, went back into the kitchen drawer. I tried to doctor that unlucky Fido—what the heck happened? Will this kindness mean a checkmark on God's tablet? Or, because my sins are many, will He return to the river's bank for more mud to shape into more tablets? Or will he just haul off and throw the mud at me?

Give me 120 years, dear God. I plan to write really good poems. And I anticipate not one *Collected Poems*, but three or four. Maybe, over this long lifespan, I'll finally win a prize to nail onto a bedroom wall. There will be controversial biographies (was he or was he not gay?), schools named after me, maybe a sitcom. The president will call to inquire about my health. My hearing aid, having fallen into a glass of water, will offer up a single bubble in response.

I'll sigh for my poet friends, all departed, some-where up in the trees, or maybe in a cloud that goes around the planet wetting people. My wife will be gone, but the numerous photos of her in my house will follow me. "Gary," her eyes will say, "aim better. You're splashing the toilet!"

Retired, with a limp that drags me in a circle, I'll do as I please. I'll visit the rose garden. I'll grow succulents in coffee cans, comb my cat for the last migratory flea. I'll cut coupons and paste them into an album to remind myself, over cold cereal, of the money that I didn't spend. I'll sleep, I'll wake, I'll sleep again with socks on my hands. Why, I won't know.

The last year of my 120 will be solitary, in preparation for the vault where they'll fit me in a receptacle. But first there will be death. I'll brace myself for the exit of light from my closed eyes, and they'll slip slightly open to see if it's really all over.

BIOGRAPHY READING

WILLIAM FAULKNER was stationed in front of the Plaza Hotel in New York, somewhere at the end of the 1930s, with money in his pocket, with an unlit pipe in his hand, with pencil lead on his tongue from biting the point, to get it going. He was waiting for an acquaintance, doing nothing really, when a child in a tiny sailor dress tripped, fell, and began to cry. His gaze lowered as he assessed the situation: girl crying, girl with skinned knees, a palm bleeding, lacy white socks. A shoe was off her foot. As Faulkner took a step back, three women rushed dutifully to help the child.

Faulkner's acquaintance, getting out of a cab, witnessed the incident. He noticed that Faulkner had stood stork-like, polishing his shoe on the back of his pants leg. The acquaintance apologized to Faulkner for his lateness and, when they started toward a restaurant on Ninth Avenue, asked, "Didn't you see the girl fall?" The novelist glanced at his friend. Pipe in his mouth, he mumbled, "Oh, yes, the child." He maneuvered along the crowded sidewalk, enduring the small injuries of shoulder bumps, stepped-on shoes, pokes from umbrellas, mutters of passersby with large bags, cabs honking at all comers.

Poets and writers are engaged in the larger fall.

THOUGH WE STARTED OUT NEW

ANOTHER STOLEN CAR rolls slowly into the Mendota Canal, the V-8 under its hood hissing a toxic anger. Geese waddle over—a web-footed gang that honks and rakes their beaks like swords under their wings. The car sinks only so far, a Raider Nation flag on the antenna. The keys are in the ignition, the dash dead of time and music. French fries rise from the mats and float like canoes.

If you're the greasy-haired biker who drove the car there, if you're the ex-brother-in-law, if you're the welterweight with a flattened nose . . . we all end up like that car: lights out, half-submerged in muck, gas tank gurgling foul water.

A dog on a trail to no good wades into the water, drinks sloppily. Next spring he will father pups with sightless eyes. The frogs with five legs will testify in the courtyard of yellowish reeds.

The sun sizzles on the state-maintained canal, and the moon, bitten by the teeth of a very old god, takes over. It's then the poets show up.

BOOK SIGNINGS

I'VE RELINQUISHED MY ROLE as poet in the Bay
Area. I cringe at the suggestion of participating in
public readings. I don't involve myself in writing con-
ferences, mentoring, bookstore signings, or answering
letters that involve questions like, "Where do you get
your ideas?" I've failed in all of these.

I revisit two occasions: the first in San Francisco,
where I read poems about our daughter, Mariko, then
age nine. Sensing that I wasn't reaching the audience—
all fourteen in folding chairs—I read next about
Fresno and straight-ahead Highway 99. I made refer-
ences to working in fields, to Cesar Chavez, canals, and
pesticides. I failed so totally in reaching my audience
that some of them got up and walked away, across the
dirty carpet and into a dirty street (the bookstore was
on Valencia).

At the end—there was an end, thank God—a
Chicano with a droopy, gray-tinted mustache rose
like King Kong and with a wrench-thick finger asked,
"What has been your contribution to *Chicano* literature?" The tattoos on his throat jumped, and spit actually shot out of his mouth. Hatred blew across the room.
Hatred because I was wearing a new wool coat and my
shoes were not scuffed by hard living? I swallowed a
mouse of fear, noticing that the remaining crowd was
small enough to fit in a van. My spine straightened.

I answered, "I'm the first Chicano to write in complete sentences, *ese.*"

We poets will stir up hate, and confirm rumors that we are untamable loudmouths, drunks, hit-and-split artists. ("Hey, you got my check? I got to go.") We try to bolster our egos by telling ourselves that the world is stupid. We survive on silence, as if we're wearing Bose headgear 24/7.

Second, I recall my pal Gerry Haslam, fiction writer and essayist, and our pairing at Barnes & Noble in Jack London Square in Oakland. It seemed an appropriate pairing, Gerry from Bakersfield and me from Fresno. Gerry suggested dinner. Dinner with Gerry and his wife, and my wife on my arm? I couldn't say no to that. Dinner was Chinese that evening, something like famine relief, the lazy Susan spinning like a merry-go-round. We scraped every last noodle onto our plates, had orange slices and fortune cookies for dessert.

We strolled from the restaurant to the bookstore, lit brightly as Disneyland at dusk. But unlike Disneyland, there were book lovers among the shelves. We were greeted by an assistant manager, female, whose bright face was lit like Disneyland as well. She pumped our hands and led us to the alcove where Gerry and I would wow the crowd. Two dozen chairs were set neatly in rows, but no one was in the chairs.

"We have ten minutes," the assistant manager remarked gleefully—the girl just bubbled. She looked down at one of the biggest wristwatches I have ever seen, its numbers like the top of an optometrist's eye chart. It was 6:55—we didn't have ten minutes! When the loudspeaker called, she hurried away in long scissoring steps.

My eyes roamed over to Gerry, who looked at me, each of us thinking, Oh, one of *those* evenings. By this we meant a small crowd, with one or two people ambushing us with a multipart question. But this evening would be different, as we soon learned.

The assistant manager returned. I could see by her watch that it was now after seven. She suggested that people were having a hard time parking. In minutes, though, they would come through the door, lots of them, some jogging and with reasonable excuses for their tardiness. She painted this Rockwell portrait with a smile.

At fifteen after, Gerry and I positioned ourselves at the front of the alcove, neither of us happy but both of us resolute. Our wives had drifted over to the magazine racks (my wife would be the one thumbing through a fashion magazine). Gerry outlined, only to me, his plan for a biography of S. I. Hayakawa. I provided him with the libretto of *Nerdlandia*, which would be performed at high schools in the Los Angeles area the following year. We continued detailing our writing projects to each other until our audience appeared—in the shape of a gentleman in an overcoat. His appearance silenced us. Minutes had been scrubbed from our lives—what should we do now? I could feel the man staring at our backs. Five minutes marched off the clock, then the gentleman tapped Gerry's shoulder. He asked, "When does it start?"

When does it start?

Understanding my cue, I stood up swiftly, took my place behind a skeletal podium, like a game-show host, and with my *New and Selected Poems* in hand, announced, "An early poem of mine." I saw a need in the gentleman's face for poetry. I thought, OK, I'll give him poetry. I fanned a few pages, creating a wind resembling applause. I turned to a short poem called "The Gold Cannon," an unfamiliar and strange effort about the death of my father. I licked my lips and began. I was tripping horribly through the second stanza when the gentleman waved a hand and said, "Stop, stop, I'll buy the book."

Gerry Haslam didn't read that night—or at least not his own work. The chairs remained empty and our spirits dampened. As we approached the exit, I noticed no sales staff behind the checkout counters. No one was buying books on this clear autumnal evening, and no one was reading. The big clock on the wall read 7:48. Fame had come and gone, and we were out the door.

TRANSLATING

SEVERAL YEARS AGO I was involved with Migrant Ministry and an issue involving the heat stress suffered by farm workers in the San Joaquin Valley. I was asked by Ana Rizzo, an advocate assigned to the western states, to find a church to test the public's response—farm workers were no longer in the news, though they still did all the work.

I visited several churches in Oakland and Berkeley. Some of the clergy were interested, others not. The pastors and priests were not cold or indifferent. They listened, but they had their own social initiatives and Migrant Ministry wasn't part of them.

Eventually the Good Shepherd Lutheran Church in Berkeley agreed to invite farm workers to speak. Two rank-and-file members of the United Farm Workers met me on a Sunday morning, along with a Cal Berkeley student by the name of Fatima. The service was sparsely attended, with a baby crying softly, and then not so softly. As an endnote to the hour-long service, we were allowed ten minutes to speak to the congregation. I helped translate one speaker's remarks, while Fatima translated the other worker's story. Both were Mexican males. The congregation was sympathetic; during the social hour following the service, a few asked what they could do. The answer was nothing: Migrant Ministry was just testing the response of the worshipping public.

The two farm workers, Ysidro and Geronimo, were both quiet as smoke, copper-colored from field work, and gentle. This is what I especially recall, their gentleness, with handshakes that offered no pressure. After the service, I took them to a Thai restaurant off Telegraph Avenue that offered picnic tables with umbrellas. Flower baskets hung from posts and music could be heard coming from inside.

I brought a wallet filled with twenties. They, in turn, brought the earth in the folds around their eyes, under their fingernails, in the small pores on their faces. These were the faces of the underpaid and the overworked. Ysidro and Geronimo had crossed the border a number of times at Nogales and Juarez. They had waded through rivers, climbed hills, hidden behind rocks, gotten sick from the desert heat, been transported in rattling trucks—all this in order to work for pay just better than minimum wage. Geronimo had two children, both girls. Ysidro was single but said he would like to marry. He was too shy to look at Fatima when he made this comment.

Fatima asked about their work, their least favorite, their most favorite. Some believe that farm workers don't like their work. This is not true. It's the conditions after work—six men in one room and the lack of privacy. Then there are the deductions from pay, the early hour when they must rise to get ready for work, the loneliness and separation from family, and the seasonal schedule that leaves them with nothing to do from November through January. While I didn't specifically ask these workers, I also suspect that it is unpleasant to consider that their hard work is seldom understood as a contribution to our nation. Finally, farm workers are perpetually tired, whether they recognize it or not.

"I worked roses in Watsonville," Yisdro said, pointing at the red rose in a slender vase on our picnic table. "I didn't like them and they didn't like me." He was finishing his pad thai, his fork beneath the last ticker tape–size noodle. Roses are pretty, he told us, but pretty things bite.

Geronimo said that he liked picking apples. He said a brother and two cousins were in Yakima, Washington, picking apples and would stay there during the winter. He said that it was cold there, but nice when you're with a brother.

How did we get to this point, the four of us, each with our plate empty? What road, what sharp turn, what desert do we cross to a new life? When we departed, I shook hands with both Ysidro and Geronimo, the force of each man's grip so light that they've stayed with me a long time.

KEEPING ALIVE

FOR SAMUEL JOHNSON, home was often the tavern, at least during the day. His place of honor was a chair by the fire—"the throne of human felicity." The fire lit his large and unhandsome face, its flames danced in his pupils. An uncommon wit, Johnson held court, bantering with a mix of lowbrows and highbrows. When he had to relieve himself (he was partial to wine, though also drained multiple cups of tea) he aimed at a bowl in the corner, one so pungent with other patrons' urine that he might have winced at the smell, as if in pain. Or, if not the bowl, he might have used the street, his hand screening his member. Do I have literary history right? That he was once relieving himself when a washerwoman scolded, "Dr. Johnson, shame, shame! Your dick is sticking out!" In mid-stream, he turned and quipped, "Woman, don't flatter yourself. It's only hanging!"

Taverns and coffeehouses: these were his homes, his universities, and perhaps his places of worship, sanctified by the incense of wood smoldering on grates. Candles sputtered on tables, and windows rattled from carts rolling on the cobbled street. Dogs slept off their hangovers in corners; they too were partial to drink, their poison good old-fashioned ale.

Johnson arrived in London in mid-March 1737 with Davy Garrick, on a hired horse—one man rode the horse while the other kept up on foot. They had alternated back and forth—Johnson on the horse, then Garrick on the horse—all the way to London Town, where they quickly parted. Each had his own destiny in front of him.

Johnson is famous for the quip, "If you have tired of London, you have tired of life." I'm not certain if he agreed with this sentiment in his early days, or even his later days—he probably made the comment after receiving a commission from a publisher. London was loud, dangerous, and filthy, but also the place to be. I recall a scene in James Boswell's biography when the great man, with another impoverished scholar in tow, fretted the night away by walking London's streets, the engines of their exertion keeping them warm. They had no place to bunk, no table on which to lower their heads for sleep, no fire over which to rub their hands for heat. They walked until the sounds of carts and horses on the cobbled streets began again, an indication that the taverns would soon open, near daybreak. How Johnson must have sped to the hearth when he first entered an establishment, so grateful for the warmth of its friendship.

Gabriel García Márquez faced poverty in mid-1950s Paris. He survived at least one week in an unheated attic, without either cold or hot food, a tap in a corner basin the only place to quench his thirst. Years later he told his friend José Font Castro how he ate out of a garbage can in the street—no, let's be accurate: He had been at a party and, since he had no better place to go, lingered long after the other guests had departed. The host asked him to help clean up. As he washed glasses, pots, and plates, did he eye food scraps all the while? Perhaps he took them, on a large platter, to the garbage bin in the street, and there—to hell if passersby were looking—he ate those scraps, the noodles slithering into his mouth. And why waste the precious chunks of cheese, the crackers, the olives, the half-torn baguette? García Márquez was a survivor. Perhaps there was some bitterness in his description of the incident to Mr. Castro. "I was so hungry," he said, "that I salvaged what I could from the garbage, and I ate it there and then."

It was also in Paris that García Márquez sang for his meals. This was at L'Escale, a Latin American club. He sang Mexican *rancheras*—*qué gacho, hombre*—and earned a dollar per night. So does the master not only create magic on the page, but also belt out songs? How were the tips, if any? When you're really down and out, you sometimes have to sing, I guess.

Must you starve to become a poet or writer? For high art, the spoons must be put away. I conjure up the frijoles in a black pan on a low flame. Rick, the artist, and I, the poet, survived, even thrived, neither of us losing weight, as beans are protein. An orange tree stood in the courtyard of our dilapidated six-unit apartment complex, so we had vitamin C to boot. I recall snagging oranges all winter until only a few were left, like Christmas ornaments, near the top of the tree. We eventually got those too, our fingers digging hungrily into the peel and its scented mist.

IN ELEVENTH-CENTURY ENGLAND, when a king knighted a soldier or other loyal citizen of the realm, he placed a kiss on the left cheek, followed by the recitation, "In the name of the Father, the Son, and the Holy Ghost, I make you a knight." This was after a sword had been presented to the honoree, a mantle had been draped over shoulders, a belt looped around the waist, and spurs fitted on armored shoes. In Germany the scene was similar: all the goodies, a kiss on one cheek, then a roundhouse bash to the other—to remind the recipient of hard knocks to come.

Poets should receive their own goodies—pencil and paper—along with the kiss, the bash on the side of the head, and another in the snout, just to make sure they understand. And the poet's steed? A bicycle with bent rims, to further remind them the going is slow.

MORE OF THE SAME

AFTER A TWO-HUNDRED-MILE DRIVE, a poet friend flops his backside onto my couch. He covers his face with one hand and produces a sigh that does nothing to improve his inner state. He rests in this manner, then asks for a beer. The domestic brand arrives, uncapped. The beer is brought to his mouth.

"What's wrong?" I ask, after he has caught his breath (and most of the beer has disappeared down his gullet).

"Last night I went to the worst poetry reading I've ever been to," he remarks. He sips the remaining brew, sneers at the label on the bottle, bright as a medal. He looks at me, eyes red as crayons, and says, "And I'm the one who gave it."

Been there. At least my compadre got to read his poetry. I reshuffle the experience at Barnes & Noble, Gerry and me, hotshots without an audience.

Why read your work in public? I've given up, at least in the Bay Area, where it seems that every third citizen, burned by divorce or still smoldering from childhood pain, is writing a book on their laptop. And once the book is written—no, once the book is published—you want others to know about it. This means bookstores, literary festivals, libraries, schools, and community colleges—even juvies, where only paperbacks are allowed, since hardbacks are considered lethal. I know this from personal experience. Before I could talk to the incarcerated youth about the beauty of reading, I had to surrender the hardcover edition to a guy in a red windbreaker.

Poetry, obviously, has an oral tradition. "Like, duh," a third-year English major might say. It can be read theatrically, provided it's not melodramatic. There is nothing worse than bad acting—we see enough of this in politicians. But some poets, showboats at heart, can't help themselves. They'll read their poems so crazy loud, with so much hand-waving and so many facial gestures that you, the audience, are forced to look down at your shoes, embarrassed by these antics.

Here's the story of a reading in a public park: A poet in tinted glasses, African beads swinging in his dread-locks. This man was reading his poetry so wildly that a homeless brother, intrigued by the rhythms, guided his shopping cart to the front of the sparse crowd. Seeing this, the poet revved up his verse, screaming his lines. I suppose he thought that he was reaching this individual, that he, master of hip-hop, slam-dunker of truly vital poetry, was stirring another soul.

When the poet finished his routine, he bowed, dreadlocks whipping over his head, the sweat like rain on his brow. Then the homeless brother approached the groovy brother. "What's wrong with you?" he asked, thinking that he had stumbled not on a poetry reading but on a person—sadder than him, crazier than him—belting out lunatic jargon.

I went on next.

THE LAST WORD

CODY'S BOOKS was founded by Fred and Pat Cody in 1956 and after several moves settled on Telegraph Avenue, three blocks south of Cal Berkeley. It was massive, with two floors and plenty of natural light in which a cheapskate browser could hunker down among books and read for free. Since it was near a major university, it was a natural to do good business, so much so that a second store (San Francisco) and a third (West Berkeley) were added in later years. I swear that the checkout stand at the Telegraph Avenue store was like Costco: buyers waiting in line, picking up tempting odds and ends as they waited, just as we do at the supermarket checkout—gee, should I buy this chocolate?

This is what I remember of Cody's Books on Telegraph, and that on the second-floor alcove, where readings took place, photos of famous and not-so-famous writers hung on the wall: Margaret Atwood and Joyce Carol Oates, for instance, among the ranks of the magisterially famous, along with President Clinton, a nonwriter, and Muhammad Ali, also a nonwriter but a champ in every way. I read there several times, a pip-squeak of a poet behind a wobbly podium. But no photo of me was ever added to the wall grouping, me or any of the many others not among the pantheon. Fuck it, I whispered to myself. Specifically, I recall reading there in the late 1970s and peddling a chapbook of mine for fifty cents—yes, five dimes, ten nickels, fifty bitter pennies, however your accountant might add it up. I sold a single copy. Why would I admit such disgrace? Did I really need that chump change? No, I was trying to make my poetry (a stapled job done in the kitchen of a friend of a friend) available to student poetry lovers.

Cody's Books harbored Vietnam War protesters of the 1970s who sought refuge from tear gas stinking up Telegraph Avenue, and Cody's adamantly displayed Salman Rushdie's *The Satanic Verses* in its windows, despite an undetonated bomb found on the store premises. Iranian clerics, as you may remember, had ordered a fatwa on Rushdie, meaning that his goose was cooked if he showed his face in public. Cody's Books was not about to be intimidated.

Let me move ahead the years, or decades. The book industry, namely independent booksellers, was faring poorly. By the mid-2000s, Cody's Books could no longer compete with Amazon.com or the discounters like Barnes & Noble and Borders. Possibly there were bad business decisions by the store management—who knows? What we do know is that Cody's began to shrink—the three locations became two locations, then just one. When the last was finally shuttered in 2007, the shelved books were reboxed and returned to the publishers, and the furniture was auctioned off.

But not all was over, however. A brand-new Cody's Books opened on Shattuck Avenue in downtown Berkeley—lots of foot traffic, lots of light and hip décor, but noticeably fewer rows of books. This resurrection in a gloomy time was cheered, though patrons recognized that the bookstore was only a shell of its original self. I recall buying a couple of books there plus a magnet with the face of Edgar Allen Poe that I placed on the face of my refrigerator, but its staying power was not evident. It slowly descended until it was near the floor.

Within months the bookstore on Shattuck Avenue closed on a moment's notice. With the front window smeared white, this institution with a history of more than fifty years was, indeed, checkmated one last time. But that didn't stop the writer who was scheduled a few days after its closure from reading his work in front of the closed bookstore. I don't know this brother writer, but he's among the best. He had heart. He arrived with his newly published book, did his own introduction to passersby, opened the pages, and began to read, stubborn as a toad because literature must be heard!

On June 24 at 7:30 in the evening, in the gusty wind of crazy downtown Berkeley, as curious bystanders stopped and stepped back to give him room, he was the novelist having the last word. As one or two heard him out to the end, I imagine that pigeons arrived. No food was forthcoming, but they did get well-formed words causing them to bob in circles and spank their wings in applause.

FLAT TIRE

MY BUDDY DAVID RUENZEL and I were crowing about Hemingway—how did his penniless characters always manage to eat and drink proper stuff?—when, in the agricultural fields ten miles east of Mendota, my car lurched to the right. My hands instinctively gripped the steering wheel. At first I thought the car had slid on tomatoes fallen off a truck, but the glowing gauge on my instrument panel showed a flat tire.

Punctured tire in the boondocks. I slowed the car with light pressure on the brakes. Gravel ticked against the fenders as I pulled over to the shoulder of the road. In the field to the right idled a large tractor with metal wings on both sides. When the machine is in operation, the wings are conveyor belts that roll cantaloupes into a bin. Workers grab the cantaloupes, box them, and stack the boxes—a swift process. I have seen the machine many times. It's efficient, like a great monster walking toward you, the inescapable thing in your nightmares.

The August dust was rolling over the car when David and I got out. Right away I understood the back right tire was the culprit. Bending down, I frisked the tire and located a nail. I stood up, mildly upset that our trip had been altered by this roadside emergency. I looked at the monster machine and its crew of ten at lunch. They huddled in the shade of the great umbrella that hung over the driver's seat, or sat against tires as tall as the workers.

We were something new. The workers stared at us, their lunchtime entertainment. Then a very boyish boy got up. He hurried over, raising his hand to his straw hat when the wind of his hustle nearly knocked it off. He turned and, in Spanish, shouted to his *jefe* that he was going to help us. He continued high-stepping over the cantaloupes, like a football player at a workout.

"Where is it?" he asked, as he approached the trunk. He was breathless. His chest was heaving. By "it" he meant the spare.

I was glad for the eagerness of this young man. He was like me when I was nineteen, thin as a shadow. He pulled back the carpet in the trunk and brought out the tire—it looked as small as a Cheerio compared to the others. He located the jack, tire iron, and lug wrench. Soon the car's right side was rising with each click-click of the jack.

David and I, neither of us handy, just watched the youth, now wrenching off the lug nuts, a grimace on his face from the strain. We assessed our limitations. We couldn't change an electrical outlet or a fan belt, lay bricks, or clear a drain without awful chemicals. (I have, however, climbed my roof and poked an untwisted clothes hanger into the downspouts.)

We joked that our one ability was taste. We could taste enchiladas, lasagna, and chicken grilled Spanish-style, sizzling immodestly, legs in the air, on a spit. We could judge fruit—two bites of an organic Fuji apple and we'd have something to say. We could assess salsa and might even chime in with a thought or two about the texture of meatloaf. We could taste drinks: "That beer is, like, really cold and good. I'll have another."

Actually I was untruthful when I said I wasn't handy. Tires I can do. Once I worked in a tire factory, at a machine where I buffed whitewalls white again.

On that warm August afternoon, dressed in a clean linen outfit, I could have struggled with this emergency, but the wonderful young man had come to my rescue. We left him to his work, David now talking about Steinbeck, whose characters were often as poor as Hemingway's characters but seldom ate or drank. What was it about Hemingway's oral fixation?

Tired of literary talk, I hovered over the young man, still on his knees. I learned that he came from a large family—six boys—and that he had just graduated from Mendota High School. I told him I was a poet and he said, lowering the jack, "Oh, I know who you are. You're Gary Soto."

David and I looked at each other.

The young man said that he had heard me at a school assembly. He recalled the story of my first girlfriend, Lupita, and my bicycle date with her, how I didn't have enough leg strength to propel the bike, so we had to change places. I got on the crossbar and Lupita, a soccer player with muscled calves, pedaled me. The bike had done wheelies from the strength of her pedaling. I was amazed that he remembered my little jokes.

I gave the boy forty dollars. We shook hands, an oily grime pressing into my palm, grime that might suggest I had changed a tire. I waved to the *jefe*, who had allowed the young man to help us, even though lunch was over and the workers were moving at a quick pace alongside the great monster tractor. Black plumes coughed from a tall exhaust pipe. The Mexican flag waved in the wind.

From Mendota to Fresno, David and I talked Steinbeck, novelist of farm workers, these specters we see from the road. Up close, of course, we see people better.

NOW WHO SAID THAT?

THE SCENE COULD HAVE BEEN from a Wodehouse or
Beerbohm biography, but definitely not from the history of John Gielgud or Somerset Maugham. Or it could
have been tucked in a book about Evelyn Waugh, but
certainly not in any of the dozen sturdy biographies
of Winston Churchill. The incident I'm searching for
is set in England, around the 1920s, for I recall spats,
tails, and beaver-fur top hats, attire from the Gatsby
era, but in London. I'm sure it was London. I recall
lamplight, fog, a tugboat moaning on the Thames.
Was the sipping of champagne involved? Did a butler
appear from behind a large door and ask, stiffly, "You
rang, m'lord?"

I require a small dose of laughter from time to time,
and I want it this morning. Here's what I'm looking for:
A recently married novelist has a new wife (his second) who is always ordering him to "shut up." "Shut
up" at breakfast. "Shut up" before he departs in his
puny Morris. "Shut up" as he reaches for his Scotch,
two inches of amber light in a crystal tumbler. The
wife is a scold, though thin as a tulip, pretty, and a
nice complement to the furniture. Day after day, she
berates her husband. She repeats this verbal directive
so often that the maid, a German fräulein, believes
that the husband's first name is "Shut Up." The maid

is busy with her duster, busy making the bed, busy beating rugs against a wall outside the house. Shut Up seems a gentleman to her. What's the beef?

That's all I'm asking for, the name of the novelist, henpecked fellow in spats, the one who waves away the cigar smoke in fear when his wife enters the parlor. No, I'm not henpecked, but I do feel a little down and in need of laughter. I've received an e-mail rejection from yet another literary magazine in the Midwest. And to think I was going to subscribe.

LETTERS

SEVERAL YEARS AGO I received a pleasant call from a teacher from a Central Valley town in California. She was giggling and I was giggling. Both us of were almost loopy—she from talking to me, a children's writer, and I from having witnessed, an hour or two earlier, an Irish setter eating an apple while sitting shotgun in a ragtop VW (this is true, dear reader, and worth a comment somewhere else).

The teacher asked whether I did school presentations. The answer was yes. When she asked about my presentations—length and subject—I told her about my storytelling skills and said that most schools were happy when I stuck a hand out of my car for a goodbye wave. When she asked what kind of student I would like to speak to—grade levels, she meant—I told her the higher grades, meaning fourth grade on up. I also told her that I would appreciate students who were attentive, respectful, on the same page, etc.

We hung up. I went back to completing a poem about a dog eating an apple, which I aptly titled "True Story." The poem begins with me in a gloomy mood after having received a form rejection from a literary magazine in the Midwest that no one has ever heard of. I walk around Berkeley until I come across a comic scene brought on by this dog. The dog rescues me from gloom when he drops some of the apple, steaming with his slobber, into the street. The ruins of the apple are meant for me—eat up.

I soon heard back from the school in the Central Valley, but not from the teacher who had called, nor the principal. Had my choice of the word "attentive" been twisted like a paper clip? Or was it the word "respectful"? Did someone have it in for me? I asked these questions because I received thirty student letters. The first began, "I was told that you only want to meet with the high kids when you visit our school. What you are doing is unfair to the kids that are struggling. I think you are prejudice you hurt kids feeling and you make feel stupid and left out. Some people ain't as high at the same thang . . . I also know you grew up in a poor neighborhood in Fresno. Did you have good grades when you were in school. Your makings kids feel bad about them selves by doing this. So you probably think the smart kids better than the lower kids . . ."

I set the letter aside and opened another envelope. This one was identically composed—dictated by the teacher using a whiteboard? A blackboard? Did she write this letter, then clap her hands of chalk? Suddenly those poems rejected by a literary magazine seemed unimportant. And where was the dog juggling an apple in his chops? Where was happiness?

These letters were written in 2004. I've since driven past that Central Valley town but have not bothered to stop.

HERB CAEN MOMENT

MR. CAEN, the *San Francisco Chronicle* journalist, was known for his three-dot column, meaning that he ended each snippet with three dots, as in . . . His thrice-weekly columns would share funny yarns and were infallibly engaging. His work suggested that life contains ellipses, not unlike, I suppose, a hospital patient hooked up to a monitor: He's sick and has been sick for a while. Then the monitor suddenly lets out a screech. The three dots become a line of dots—and he's gone.

Caen entertained while he provided insight into human follies. A few of his columns have stayed with me. Example: A billionaire computer type is giving a party at a swank resort in Napa. On check-in a visitor is told that, at ten o'clock in the evening, Mr. Billionaire will provide for his guests an awesome display of fireworks. The visitor, signing his name in the guestbook (passé these days), didn't bother to meet the receptionist's eyes. He tells the person behind the counter, "Oh, that's nice—fireworks for his guests. I promise I won't look."

Another example: A family of three—dad, mom, and son—is having dinner at a four-star restaurant. Mom asks the son, age four and dressed in a child's blazer, what he would like to drink with his meal. He looks thoughtfully around at the other diners, turns back to his mother, and says, "A glass of Chablis." The mother smiles and says, "No, no, we can't have wine in public." At that, the boy sighs. He again lets his eyes patrol the other diners before he makes his call: "OK, a cup of coffee—black."

Mr. Caen wasn't around for this: A famous film director flies to France and, darn it, he has forgotten two bottles of a delectable red, some smoky bullshit with a swimmingly fat-ass body. He could have smacked his brow with the flat of his palm and ended it at that. But he is throwing a party for chums in a fortnight! He can't disappoint. As a daddy with mucho zeros on the end of a nine, he is of the kind who understands, with the help of his accountant, the tax write-off. He hires a private jet to fly over these bottles of wine, each buckled in, I imagine, each jostled through a spate of turbulence over the North Pole, but each arriving safely. As they were bottles, not people or other living creatures, they weren't forced to go through customs. I suspect that they were poured and, after a secondary swirl in a large wine glass, nonsense was issued over the bullshit.

We've all spent money foolishly. I once bought a bottle of pinot noir for fifty dollars and strapped it into the passenger's seat. The ride home was only six blocks, but I wasn't about to take a chance on that baby.

A BAY AREA LITERARY PRIZE

IN 1997 I FORMED a small book distribution company called Soto & Friends, a move that made one San Jose children's bookstore grumble, "You're cutting off your nose!" By that outburst, she meant that if I were distributing my own books, she wouldn't stock my titles. Her argument? I was taking business from her store. Oh, that hurt; that made me bleed. I promised myself the next time I saw her I would wear a Band-Aid on my snout.

Snarky, I admit.

As you might guess from the name, I also envisioned distributing books published by friends but grew apprehensive at the prospect of storing their titles, a whole warehouse of them, none of which moved, titles without legs to run into the arms of book buyers. Still, since the name had been registered with the state of California, I couldn't change it without paperwork. My entrepreneurial idea changed, the name remained.

I was packing books of mine—Merced County had purchased several hundred copies of three different titles—when I received a call from a frenzied person representing a Bay Area literary group. He informed me that my 2007 short-story collection, *Facts of Life*, was a finalist for their annual book award. I put down my tape gun, my breathing heavy not from excitement but from the effort of lifting three boxes, one after another, onto my wife's workstation in our office. I had been packing hardbacks.

"Say that again?" I asked.

He repeated himself, more slowly the second time around. He padded his conversation with expectations of a large book-buying crowd.

I was aware of this literary group and its prize, which was a certificate—no cash, not even free alcohol at the reception. I touched my nose, which had grown back splendidly, if not more aquiline. I wondered if I were about to cut off my nose again. I had been among the finalists on two other occasions. Each time I had appeared at the ceremony in full regalia (suit and tie), but driven home a bridesmaid, a nonwinner—oh, let me say it—a loser. As a loser, I had to applaud the winner and use massive energy to hoist a smile. (I learned later, from a three-time finalist in adult fiction, that the committee informs the winners in advance, so that they might be prepared to articulate their happiness, etc.)

On this, my third time around, I asked the caller for the date. Bad actor that I am, I said, "Let me check my calendar." I held the phone down at my side, counted to six, then raised the phone. "I'm sorry," I said, "but I'm not available. Darn!" I checked my nose—it was still present.

"Are you sure you can't postpone what you're doing?" The caller—a committee member, I learned—had become stubborn. Rearrange your schedule, sucker. You have to be there!

"No, no, no," I answered with a voice empty of truth. "A friend is getting married." This was a fat lie. If I'd said that a friend was getting divorced, that would've been closer to reality. The caller tried once more, but without much heat in his words. Finally, he asked, "Do you have someone who can represent you?"

"Represent me?"

"Stand in for you?"

The wheels inside my head turned. A picture of a drinking buddy appeared at the back of my mind. "Yeah, this buddy of mine, name of David Ruenzel." David and I are the best of friends and, moreover, he owed me one—I had served a restraining order on a minor (asshole teenager, with stupidity for brains) who had been harassing the Ruenzel family by throwing rocks at their house, late at night.

Without shame, the caller asked if the committee could have an extra copy of my book—the presenter needed one. At that, I blinked, concluding that I was certainly not a contender. They didn't even have the book! I should have answered with a frosty no. But I looked at my tape gun, nearly depleted of tape. Business had been good.

"Yeah, I can get you one."

I met the presenter—a poet and editor of an occasional literary magazine—at the UPS store on Solano Avenue. We knew each other, vaguely, and I kept it that. I gave her the book and excused myself, braying, "I've got to ship all these books." I hooked a thumb at the boxes in the bed of my truck. They were off to

Merced, where they would be read by children sitting in swings—or so I imagined.

As the ceremonial date got closer, I phoned David and reminded him that he didn't have to show up early. The first part of the ceremony involved milling about—he wouldn't find it of much interest. I told him to arrive midway.

Wrong.

That year, the award presentations were the first order of business, so no one represented me when the finalists went up to the stage. The MC apparently called David's name several times. I imagine that the audience looked around, confused. Where was this fellow David Ruenzel? Was his hearing aid turned off? Was he in the john?

There were five finalists in my category: young people's literature. There were four on the stage, standing shoulder to shoulder, when the winner was announced. Three returned to their seats, holding onto the railing on their way back. I wasn't the winner, the one with the acceptance speech up his sleeve. In fact, at the time of the announcement, I was playing pickup hoops at Codornices Park in Berkeley, with my team of old jocks, none decorated, leading us toward a lopsided loss—yet another day in my life.

YOU DON'T HAVE TO READ
ANY FURTHER

I RECEIVED AN ENVELOPE that contained twenty-four letters from third graders in Stockton, California. The letters were perfumed with the artificial smell of crayons. The letters blossomed smiley faces, arching rainbows, bright suns, sunflowers, and lopsided houses. How sweet, I thought, a proper drink in my paw, and revisited in memory my visit to the Stockton school, where I had spent the day spinning from the air stories that produced wholesome mirth. I picked up the first letter. It read, "Thanks for coming to our school to sell your books." Sell your books, I repeated under my breath, the ice cube in my drink cracking from the global warming of my hand. I sipped my amber drink, and I sipped again. Was this kid a wisenheimer? Was this the sum of my appearance at the Stockton school? I shared the letter with my wife. She smiled and said, "The kid is spot-on smart."

A LIBRARY IN SOUTH FRESNO, and me doing a little freebie talk to fifth graders from a nearby school. The kids are on the floor, legs folded, their backpacks along the wall. They are fairly attentive, nice even, though the scent of artificially flavored Cheetos in the closed room is overwhelming. I spout a few stories (some laughter, some glimmers) and read from my Christmas book, *Too Many Tamales*. I also read from *Chato's Kitchen*, which features a low-riding cat and his carnal (sidekick), Novio Boy. After twenty minutes of presentation, I prod the students for questions. There is a sigh of appreciation, as they understand that this thing is almost over. Soon they can go out and play.

One asks, "Where do you get your ideas?" I roust from memory the salted rim of a margarita glass but refrain from offering this image. I say ideas come like magic, a little black smoke, and there it is, a book. Huh? I answer other questions: "Who does your illustrations?" "Do you have children?" "Do you want more children?" "Do you have cats if you write about cats?" "Are you super rich or super famous?" Finally, I entertain a question from a kid who, I've noticed, has been squirrelly on the floor and bothering classmates. He has bangs that almost hide his eyes. He stands up, hoisting his pants, which are punched with holes at the knees. He asks, "You used to go out with my mom, huh?"

I look at this little beast, my eyes beady with curiosity. A few seconds stretch into a full minute. He does look familiar.

THE GOLD STANDARD

CHEMISTS AND POETS clock in at the same lab. We work in separate stations to mix raw materials for the greater good. In 1675 a German chemist named Hennig Brand had deduced by whimsy that human urine could be distilled into liquid gold. He arrived at this simply because urine resembled gold—in color, that is. From bladder-filled friends, Professor Brand collected buckets of the stuff and even recruited a platoon from the German army, all drinkers, to add to his reserves. In his lab he did a little of this and a little of that and produced a pasty substance that glowed. He assigned a name to this glowing paste: phosphorous. No gold, however, was forthcoming; no alchemy and hocus-pocus made him richer. It was valueless paste that burned brightly when lit, after-dinner entertainment, perhaps, for guests.

When a Swedish chemist named Karl Scheele in the 1750s came upon Brand's recipe, he grew curious, entrepreneurial. He collected vats of urine from many sources. He allowed the liquid to distill before he blended his own paste—again phosphorous and again unprofitable. Scheele failed to make phosphorous in abundance, which could have made his venture viably commercial. In time, though, he got it right. He abandoned urine as an ingredient and made a substitution (an industry secret, I'm afraid). Very quickly, Scheele discovered a commercial application: matches. A bright light was born. To this day, Sweden is still one of the leading manufacturers of matches.

I'm thinking of this scientific history because perhaps the early chemists should have blown a mighty trumpet for poets, all heavy drinkers, all freeloaders when it comes to grog. We poets could have supplied enough urine—and certainly bullshit, if needed— to make phosphorous a winning operation from the get-go. I've seen poets drink, and I have been a poet with my own pissy brew. I like beer and I like wine. I've looked up late at night at the stars, my zipper undone. I've staggered to a country tree and created my own river after drinking some really cheapo shit. O stars and heaven! I've wept. O seas! O seesaws! O sandwiches! (Huh?)

Soldiers from any land are teetotalers compared to us, we of Dylan Thomas and Malcolm Lowry, we of John Berryman and Anne Sexton. We could produce great vats of sour swill to boil down. Once the paste was ready, we could dab it on the end of our poet's pencil to produce one bright flare of smelly light.

A AGA

THE SMALLEST BOOK in my poetry collection is written—no, dictated and illustrated—by Jake Gordon Young, son of Gary Young, poet and printer. It measures three inches by four inches and has a collector's quality to the production: handset Garamond type, handmade paper called Umbria, hand-bound in green cloth, with a decorative label, tiny as a square of confetti, on the spine. The label reads, *A Aga*. Published in 1992, there are seventy-five such first-edition copies in the world. It's short on stature when placed next to *The Poetry of Pablo Neruda*. Still, if Neruda were alive, he might take a look at it, read it in less than a minute, and pronounce it a rare beginning.

It is rare and it is a beginning. Master Jake dictated this book when he was just out of Pampers. His father told me the manuscript was created in New York, while Jake was suffering the deliriums of mononucleosis. At three years old, the child was already experiencing a Rimbaud moment. He lay in bed, sweaty from fever, and yet, art was on his mind. When his father asked, "Can I get you anything?" the child responded, "Ink and paper."

The storyline of *A Aga* is classic: A very good fellow is riding a horse and comes upon bad dudes doing bad-dude things. The good fellow slaughters them. With permission, I quote a passage:

I saw another bad guy
and stabbed him
in his heart
his chest
his whole body

There are other such passages, including one about a deer that is eaten by the narrator and a new sidekick from the forest. In the end, the narrator (OK, Jake) finds a girl and lives happily ever after with her.

I plucked this book from the shelf a couple of days ago—actually, it slipped off the shelf when I was pulling out Neruda's collected poems, Neruda with his big, hardbound body of work. I was excited by my discovery. I ran a finger across the cover to dispense with the dust and read the entire collection, leaning against my bookshelf. The narrative was so compact that I read it again, this time lingering on the drawings. I pondered the creative psyche of Master Jake and how, at age three, he was already familiar with structure—good guy on a journey, good guy confronting bad guy, good guy embracing an amigo, good guy surviving the elements; then finally, at the advanced age of twenty (for Jake, twenty would have been hella old), good guy settles down with a beauty. I suspect that his father, poet and printer, had read adventure tales to him in bed—the son with a thumb in his mouth, slowly drifting off to sleep, with slaughter and mayhem playing behind his twittering eyelids.

We might think this is a cute first effort, a keepsake, a potential heirloom to show the boy when he grows into a young man with tattoos snaking up his arms. It's more than cute, though. It wasn't his first manuscript, nor his second or third. It was the result of months of practice, of drawings executed in charcoal, ink, pastels, pencil—whatever struck the boy's fancy. From what I gather, Gary would take Jake to the studio where the monstrous printing presses were kept. At first, Jake was placed in a crib while his father worked. Then the crib was removed, and a comfy chair brought in. To keep busy Jake drew and, thus, grooved creatively while the printing presses turned.

Gary Young is a poet, teacher, and fine-press printer. We first met as classmates in the MFA program at UC Irvine. Gary was a year ahead of me, a little more settled in life (married, for instance, and with an idea of what to do with his life), and had a gentle, artistic side to his character. I could judge this by his penmanship, which was artful and beautiful to behold. My penmanship was clumsy as a kid walking with Pepsi cans smashed under his sneakers.

Gary published his son's book in a limited edition, and he has also brought out other books, marvelous works, particularly those of Mallarmé. Gary's books have been collected by major museums in the United States and abroad, particularly in Japan. He and his family live in a forest (this is truth, not legend) and live close to the bone, meaning that things can be tight financially. Such is the life of a poet; for a poet and printer, it might be even rougher. He must have thought, on several occasions, of the deer in the forest, and how he might have hunted, like Jake's good guy, for his meat.

In 1993 Gary visited Chronicle Books of San Francisco, which was publishing my poetry at the time. He visited with an editor (was it Jay Schaefer?) and shared samples of his fine-press books, including a seductive masterwork of Mallarmé poetry. The editor, though, was taken by a series of relief prints. Here was a coffee-table book, the editor must have thought, for discerning book collectors. The editor was keen on publishing one of Gary's books. However, after the numbers were crunched and swallowed, the publisher opted out of the series of relief prints, tentatively titled *Geography of Home*. It was too rich a project.

The editor then asked, "Do you have something smaller?" To answer that question, Gary pulled out *A Aga*, possibly from his coat pocket. Chronicle Books, enchanted by its size and authorship, published the pint-sized book a year later. Jake was in kindergarten by then, filling his shoes with sand by jumping up and down in the sandbox. His advance was five thousand dollars. With that princely sum, he could have bought his classmates ice cream for a year!

The book sold modestly. And Jake grew up to be a poet. Once the slayer of bad guys, he is currently completing an MFA in creative writing. On his graduate school application, Jake Gordon Young provided *A Aga* as evidence of publication.

LONDON CALLING

ON THE MILLENNIUM BRIDGE, London, I leaned over the rail and cast my eye on the Thames, gray as oil. In fact, the river is partly oil, from passing ships, tourist barges, and tugboats. It's an old, troubled river, one that winds like an intestinal tract toward the sea. The river has carried ships, small and large, of wood and of iron, along with sludge of every sort—factory waste, human waste, animal waste, chemical waste that glows in the dark—and the suicidal tears of the heartbroken. The Romans appeared on its banks, and the Vikings and the Normans, as well as immigrants from Africa, China, India, Pakistan, and the Middle East. The river has suffered from fires and plagues, from mercenary troops on its many bridges. It has ferried slaves, prisoners, reluctant soldiers, sailors from many nations, kings and queens and serpents, even fish, thin as playing cards. Corpses have knocked against its wharves, as have bloated horses and cows. It has held the reflections of stars and moons in all their cycles, and has accepted rain, piss, vomit, and grog, including my own contribution, a warm splash of Foster's from a can I was clutching. For the moment, I was done drinking. I poured the contents into this slow river.

I hopped onto the District Line to Earl's Court, where I debarked and found the international call station, run by Pakistani brothers. The place is a miracle: you enter a booth and, for fifty cents a minute, you can call almost anywhere in the world. According to the large clock on the wall, it was 5:47 a.m. in California. Jon Veinberg, poet and friend, was house-sitting for us. An early riser, he would already be up, his coffee drunk, the paper read, our cat fed and petted. Jon picked up on the third ring. He didn't seem surprised to hear my voice.

After two minutes of chitchat—one dollar down—I asked Jon, "Did I get any calls?" I like to keep up-to-date on those thinking of me.

"You got a couple," Jon answered. "But none of them was important."

I was baffled. I asked how he could consider them unimportant. I looked up at the clock: four minutes—and two dollars—had been scrubbed from my life.

"None of them involved money."

I laughed at the snarky bastard, and Jon laughed at me, merchant at heart. I hung up before the call could cost me more.

MY TIME WITH SAMUEL PEPYS

I CARRIED *SAMUEL PEPYS*, biography by Claire Tomalin, to the shady arbor of the Berkeley Rose Garden. With one hand, I shooed crumbs from a bench and took a seat. My eyes fell on a few plates inside the book. I dreamed a little. I thought of Pepys and London: In 1640 the city was the most populous in the world—120,000 townies. Triple that for the number of rats foraging in brick-lined sewers during the day, resurfacing at night to prowl the streets. I learned there was no king that year. England was ruled by Oliver Cromwell, Lord Protector, and then he was pushed out of power when Charles II, by civil war, reclaimed the throne. By this time Pepys was a mature man, a high-ranking one, even. In present-day Great Britain, he would have been the sort of civil servant who has a car and chauffeur.

But my mental visit to old London Town was interrupted when a pigeon settled in front of me. He was a well-fed pigeon, almost Buddha-like in shape. The feathered fellow warbled when I said, "You don't know what this is, do you?" I held up Tomalin's biography—a first edition, mind you—and asked the pigeon a second time. The bird failed to supply an answer; in fact, it shuffled back a few steps at my arm movement. The large, scholarly book cast a shadow across the pebbly ground before us.

The pigeon, sensing no handout forthcoming, lifted his Buddha body into the air and went to pester a nanny at another bench. His departure allowed me to close my eyes and sigh at my good luck—to have the day to myself, this day and many like it. I imagined the Thames, the sun over the river filtered by clouds, and the ships, their sails retracted, anchored at wharves. I imagined the Tower of London, and the jewels in it, and before the jewels were there, the royal prisoners composing memoirs at stark tables. I have only to hold such an excellent book in my paws and to close my eyes, in order to call up that country. The royals called the shots. They plundered their own backyards and made war at the drop of a gauntlet. England's bloody past was ruled by tyrants who ate heartily and with their fingers. Would Charles II have eaten a pigeon? Was it a delicacy, the fine bones becoming serviceable toothpicks once the meal was over and the jester brought in?

At sixty, I'm acutely aware of my position in life: I get to read, imagining others involved in the excitement. My head will not roll and neither will my neck find itself in a noose. My causes are all inside: I wish happiness first upon myself and then on the people who surround me. I think of a poet friend who said, "I can't read while I'm asleep, and that's the truest thing I'm going to say all day."

Brilliant.

We look for truth, and truth is more often found in the highest forms of creative expression—literature, music, art. I opt for literature. My favorite novel of all time is Madame Bovary, with its cheats and its pompous clergy, the inept and the skilled, the wise and the unwise, the holy and the not-so-holy, and others, like me, on park benches, providing a colorful backdrop.

While I provide color, the principal characters with better roles stroll past. I'm an older man with a book in his hand, a character who looks up at the lovers, then looks down. I turn the pages of a very excellent book.

BE THIS FAME?

AFTER THE 1990 PUBLICATION of my book *Baseball in April*, I began to receive calls from school districts, asking me to do author presentations. I heeded these calls, especially at schools where Mexican American youths warmed almost every chair. I felt enlarged in my soul. I got to meet my readers—Raquel, Dulce, Fortino, Armando, Joel—*chavalitos* who hugged me in the hallways and sought autographs. I played it up—me, a celebrity. But inside my 133-pound frame, I shuddered—me, the fraud. After all, what was I but a poet? Poets are not supposed to have readers.

My poetry books were poor cousins to my books for young readers. *Baseball in April* was running laps around school campuses, as were my Dell-issued *A Summer Life* and *Living Up the Street*. Families started showing up at my book signings. I recall an event in my hometown of Fresno, where a little girl, hands pressed sweetly together, announced in a near whisper, "I want to be a writer too." I started to say, "Oh, sweetie, don't do that to yourself—go into engineering," but I bit my tongue.

I published a second middle-grade book, titled *Taking Sides*. The cover featured a boy with a basketball, going for a layup. A sports novel, one would easily guess. So, when I appeared at a school in Shafter,

California, the young readers had assumed that I played basketball in high school, possibly even in college. They were surprised by my average height, the gray in my hair, my lack of strength. I couldn't move the podium without the help of the librarian. Still, I had a game to play with the kids. When recess began teams were made up on the asphalt court. For the first time in my life, I was chosen first. After all, hadn't I written a basketball novel? The OG had to have something left in his tank. After a couple of embarrassing shots (at least they rang off the backboard), the kids caught on that I was no good. I recall a pixie of a girl debating whether to pass the ball to me. Her eyes locked on mine, as if she were thinking, "Should I give Mr. Soto another chance?" Then she passed the ball to a boy with unlaced shoes.

In 1991 I decided to make a film. I thought, yeah, this is where I should go. I wrote a script based on one of my stories, searched for talent, and assembled a crew, with local filmmaker John Kelly behind the camera. We made an eleven-minute film titled *The Bike*, featuring kids from Huron, California, an agricultural town, *puro Mexicano*. Once the film was completed, I argued with myself about what to do with it. The answer? Show it at the Huron Elementary School cafeteria.

Local educator Nancy Mellor helped secure the cafeteria, plus she asked the janitor to run a mop across the floor. Mothers made popcorn, sprinkled with chili powder, and overly sweet Kool-Aid. Nancy also arranged for the county fire department to lead a parade in my honor down Huron's main street. The street was lined with bars, for this was an agricultural town. (If I worked in the fields—and I have—I would tip a couple cold ones at the end of the day too.)

In 1991 Huron's citizenry numbered about three thousand. About eight hundred—anyone remotely related to the cast—joined the parade. I sat on the backseat of a customized Chevy, along with the principal actors, Rudy Martinez and Alex Garcia, both age thirteen. The other main actors (and John Kelly, the baffled cameraman) were in *el ranfla* (the car) behind us. Because of the parade's length—fire truck in the lead, red lights flashing—it began out in the grape fields. I practiced my wave on my wife, who was on the side of the road. I blew her a kiss, the cheeky husband, and formed a question on my lips: what's your number, girl?

Thus began the parade I've been enjoying ever since.

STUDENT

I WAS EXITING A GROCERY STORE with a small purchase when I recognized a former student of mine, from what, twenty-five years ago? She was getting out of her car, one long leg at a time, spiderlike. She pushed on the car door, then hip-bumped it to close it completely. She turned and saw me looking, a memory cycling through her mind and coming into focus. She took the sunglasses from the top of her head, the sunshine of her locks all gone. She came up to me, anger in her steps, and declared, "After your class, I never wrote poetry again."

I felt momentarily weak, a failure for not making poetry part of her life. She appeared hurt, even after so many years. She wasn't well-dressed. Her sweater was fuzz-balled, her shoes dull, the bangles on her wrists cheap. Unhappy, her body told me, she's unhappy. She's poor and I'm to blame. Still, I told her firmly, as if I were still her professor, "I saved you time and worry."

Had I been I trying to hurt her in class, as she was trying to hurt me now? No. It was my business to provide her with an educated critique of her writing— simple as that. She had missed the point and now here she was, still disappointed. I'm sorry she looked so bad.

She slipped on her sunglasses to dim my presence.

REPORTING ON OUR BODIES

A SCHOLAR FRIEND SAYS he left his hair in Santa Barbara and his hearing at a rock concert in Los Angeles, circa 1973. The confusion of memory began midway through *Remembrance of Things Past*. "Where in the hell are my car keys?" he asks the air. I tell him it can't be that bad—hair, hearing, and memory loss. He could be walking like a crab, with a hip replacement.

When he peels off his baseball cap, the living room suddenly shines with the glare of his naked forehead, a glare that could power a small solar panel.

"It's all gone," he laments, patting his thighs. The spring in his legs wound down in Ireland, his taste buds peeled off in Cabo, and his heart—he threw it out a window in Barstow, when his love rode away on his best Harley. He drums his fingers against the arm of the recliner. He looks down at his belly. He inhales, exhales—his exercise for the day.

"I'm fat," he claims. He says the only way he can get skinny is to die, but he won't risk going that far. He picks up his decaffeinated coffee, sips so that rivulets appear around his mouth. He says aging is not for the faint of heart. My friend is in a bad mood.

A couple hours later, at Pegasus Books on Solano Avenue in Berkeley, I'm not particularly happy either.

I'm hunkered down in the poetry section and see two of my books on the shelf: *Home Course in Religion* and *Junior College*. I open the first book to the title page, where I have personalized the copy to Claire. Who was Claire? I wonder. I open the second book, which I've apparently dedicated to Toby. Perhaps Toby was Claire's dog?

I leave the bookstore, my shadow tagging along as if it were a friend. At home I count my blessings. My teeth remain in neat rows and my knuckles continue to knock on doors—I do possess ambition. I'm thin. I'm courteous when it counts. I have a wife who loves me almost all the hours of the day.

But I do notice that the hair on my scalp has thinned and my once muscled chest is now part of my padded abs. I'm losing some of myself, piece by piece. My legs, however, still stand with me, two faithful troopers. And my talent remains: at the count of three, I can whip the horse inside me and begin down a path in search of a poem. True, it was only last week I received a rejection slip from a literary magazine in the Midwest no one has heard of, but still!

Unlike my scholar friend, who has written a book on *Moby Dick*, I won't give up. I will continue my regimen of sit-ups and duck squats down the hallway. I'll do push-ups on my fingertips again. At age sixty I have a second act, which will be performed with smoke and mirrors. I'll keep going with this heart of mine, a bulwark reinforced by every ham sandwich that I've brought to my chops. My six-pack is just below the surface—those dimples will rise again, you wait and see!

I sit in my chair next to our picture window and drum my fingers against the arm. I go to the kitchen, pour fizzy water into a tumbler, and return to my chair. I reflect, I wonder, I worry. Who was Claire? Who was Toby, man or dog?

MYSTERY

I WAS PEERING THROUGH the glittery window of a mom-and-pop jewelry store when I heard a voice say, "Like that man in the maroon jacket." I was slow, and I was dull, mainly because of my poor sleep the night before. Then the moment registered—the voice was making reference to me. I turned from the display. My eyes, once charmed by the small charms in the window, lost their luster.

The passerby was a woman in her forties, accompanied by her teenage daughter. Neither of them bothered to lift their eyes to mine, not even for a second. They were walking at a brisk clip—late for a matinee, perhaps?

The duo passed, leaving me muttering, "Like that man in the maroon jacket." I examined the vintage wool. It was maroon and stylishly vintage. Was there a stain on the front? Was the collar turned up in a funny way? Confused, I looked again at the mother and her daughter, now at the end of the street. What could she have meant?

I turned back to the window and saw my reflection: middle-aged man with combed but thinning hair, wearing slacks and a white dress shirt beneath the jacket, plus a pair of leather loafers, not the typical Berkeley trainers. I inspected my crotch: the zipper was up. I wasn't a frightening sight. If anything, I resembled an out-of-work newscaster. Why the comment then?

I walked back to my car, got in, slung the seatbelt across my shoulder, and buckled it. I judged the mother's tone of voice as brusque. Was she warning her teenager about dapper old men like me? Or was she comparing me with her new boyfriend? Could I be eye candy for older women? Or were out-of-work newscasters merely pretentious?

I drove home, hugged and kissed my wife, and relayed this little episode. She picked lint from the arm of my maroon jacket and went downstairs to her sewing room. She had no other comment except to say that there had been no phone calls while I was gone.

Evening came. We ate dinner and washed the dishes. I started to read a book in my recliner but then placed the book in my lap, my reading glasses like bent sculpture in my hands. When you have no other job, you can ponder such moments. I peeled a hangnail from one finger, felt a small stingy hurt when I came to the end of the rind. After much thought, I understood. That man in the maroon jacket was an example of someone not worth knowing.

MY TIME ON WELDON AVENUE

IN THE SUMMER OF 1973, I pushed a gas-powered mower up Weldon Avenue and stopped in front of a modest house with a scraggly lawn. I debated where to begin. I had been hired by Fresno City College to mow twenty-plus lawns, front and back, and once done to tend them until their accompanying houses and apartments, built in the 1930s, could be razed. Their time was up. The college needed offices and parking lots, and I needed a job. But until its demise, this neighborhood on the east side of the college required care. The neighborhood included an apartment I called home. There, on the building's top floor, I lived with my brother Rick, an artist; Donald Lee, a Vietnam vet and potter; and Randy Saludes, occasional college student and drummer in a Latin rock group. Our rent for the three-bedroom apartment was seventy-five dollars a month, split three ways (sometimes four, when another roommate bunked with us).

I was a grateful college student. The gardening job paid a $2.30 per hour, better than the minimum wage, which was $1.65 at the time. I had attended City between 1970 and 1972, majoring in easy classes, and was now an English major at Fresno State—a young poet with long curls like Byron. I gave this job my best. I was like the Indiana Jones of gardeners. To level the yards of tangled vines and weeds, I used a swashbuckling but dull machete. Every ten minutes I paused to rest my arms and catch my breath. It was oily work that started early in the morning and ended early in the afternoon—at three o'clock, when the Fresno sun depleted everyone's energy. For two weeks straight, I fired up that lawn mower which, I believe now, was the type responsible for global warming. It was a certified piece of junk, but I didn't complain. I got to work cleaning up the same place where I lived. What a deal, I thought. How many of us are lucky enough to mow their own lawn and get paid for it?

That summer, I lived on the water that gushed powerfully from the hose. I'd been hired in June, but the college wouldn't pay until early July. When I learned this, I asked myself, How can I survive until payday?

As it happened, I survived on love. In one of the houses (a duplex, really) dwelled a young woman whose beauty was like peeking into paradise and then going blind, her image forever etched in my memory. More than once, she came over to our place to see what we boys were doing—starving, mainly, but also making music, making art, making poetry, making our own beds and lying in them. We vagabonds subsisted on frijoles from morning to night. There were also oranges, from the tree in the yard, and grapes from a vine that ran along the fence near the railroad tracks. We were vegans before the word was coined.

I wept into my pillow over our precious neighbor. Would she ever look at me? Would she ever lock herself out of her house and give me the chance to use my head as a battering ram? I would see her come and go (she had a job, another life) and watch her wash her long, white Plymouth every other Saturday. She was beautiful, she was older, and she wasn't mine. She even had a credit card in her wallet—so that's what they're like, I remember thinking.

But I dried my eyes and regrouped. I became tactical, convinced that she would become mine when, one day, I witnessed her hammering a walnut—the shell shattered like glass. She was on her porch when I walked past, me suddenly with coins in my pocket. The college had finally paid me. I breathed in her presence, my eyelashes fluttering no doubt, as she looked up with that hammer in her hand. She smiled, then brought it down on two walnuts at once.

Strong gal, I mused. I moved down the street to Scotty's Liquor on Blackstone Avenue and returned swinging a paper bag containing a sixteen-ounce Pepsi. As the neighborhood gardener, I deserved that cold, sugary rush. I wondered how I could impress this beauty. With my wit? My good looks and long, black hair? My impressively slender waist, the result not of sit-ups but of starvation? I returned to the apartment, which overlooked her duplex. The hammering of walnuts had stopped. The young woman, Carolyn Oda, was in her kitchen. I heard the stove door open and close, then the whir of an electric mixer.

My heart thumped as I approached her duplex. I had it in mind that I could ask if there was something I could do for her. After all, wasn't I the gardener? Wasn't I responsible for seeing that our neighborhood was groomed? I climbed the cement steps, knocked, and managed to ask, "You need something?" (Was a college boy ever so young?)

She unlocked her screen door. There was something I could do: I could taste one of her cookies. I tasted one, then another, and didn't say no to a sandwich, either. My visits became daily, and I shared with her my toil at becoming a poet. She, in turn, presented me with her refrigerator. I had never seen so much food packed into such a small space. There was ham and cheese, tomatoes and lettuce, pickles and relish, jams and jellies, mustard and ketchup—the works for a boy who has just turned twenty and still has a hollow leg to fill.

Like a dog, I've been scratching at her door ever since.

PHOTOCOPYING

IN A CLASSROOM IN OREGON, I was spot-on quick, the light of cleverness illuminating my eyes like a jack-o'-lantern on a porch. I wasn't on a porch but stationed behind a table with a huge PowerPoint gizmo. To some thirty alternative high school students, I revealed the wheels and cogs of my young adult novel *Buried Onions*, wheels and cogs that I tinkered with as I went along. From my vantage point, I guessed that its narrative was relevant to them—revenge and escape from revenge, and some bloodletting on several pages to keep readers turning pages. The students were familiar with the young adult novel and could refer to its symbols, raising questions like, "Do the onions represent the tears of life?" "How come Eddie (the main character) doesn't kill the guy in yellow shoes?" "What do the yellow shoes represent?"

We enjoyed the discussion and then I was out the door—or almost out the door and into the natural light of springtime. A student approached and asked me to sign her copy of *Buried Onions*. She handed me a bound photocopied version of the book, which confused me for a moment. I lowered my eyes, now extinguished of mirth, as I grasped the situation. Nevertheless, I signed this version of my novel, all 146 pages, and added her name, Jazmine, when she asked for a personal touch. She requested this amendment twice because her pronunciation was muddled by the chrome ball attached to her grape-stained tongue. Throughout my presentation, Jazmine had been sucking a lollipop, its sweetness now gone.

A teacher came up to me, thanking me for the appearance. I pumped a handshake with him. I offered the frown of a carved pumpkin when he reported the students' enthusiasm for *Buried Onions*, which segued to my questions: You photocopied the entire sucker? All the classroom copies? His smiley face flattened, not pleased that I was questioning his teaching method— gee, I should be grateful that my literature was taught, etc. He stiffened and met my eyes. "Yes," he answered, guiltless, as he rallied his instincts for the use of literature in photocopied form. He didn't argue that the school was broke, but he did suggest as much. In turn, I wasn't about to parry his argument and say that the photocopying wasn't free—the inky heft of 146 pages must have cost something. I didn't point around the classroom and say, "Oh, yeah, Mr. Jobs gave you these Apple computers for free? And the PowerPoint arrived from a drunken Santa the day after Christmas." I wasn't about to review the many times I had seen my literary output—poems, essays, and stories—photocopied in mountainous stacks. I have argued this point in the past with no success. I just come off as a vain and stingy sourpuss.

I did my duty in springtime Oregon, in a really pretty town with tulips in every yard, hyacinths and daffodils too. I flew home with my face pressed to the window—a wagon train of clouds was heading east, filled with rain and lightning. At that altitude, 36,000 feet above it all, I debated whether I should have strongly protested the photocopying. Why hadn't I defended the rights of poets? Or defended the book, the published page—whoever shelves those ghastly college readers in their homes? What's allowable for educational jostling, what is just plain piracy that depletes the coffers of both the author and the publisher? I alert you, dear reader, of the paltry earnings of *Buried Onions*, a novel that's moving at the ground speed of a tired tortoise, not the frisky hare. I pray for your sharp math skills. For every copy sold of *Buried Onions*, I receive six percent of the seven-dollar list price, the standard percentage for paperback writers such as myself. My take of six percent per copy is forty-two cents—change to rattle in my deepest pocket. If the school had done the honorable thing— bought a classroom set of this book—I would have earned $12.60. Was that asking too much? I might have bought an overpriced sandwich and drink in the airport and, perhaps, had enough left to splurge on a magazine. The publisher, by the way, pays biannually in November and May, a long stretch between checks.

I'll call it what it is: theft of intellectual property. This activity goes on in schools from the West Coast to the East Coast, poets and writers robbed by the copy machine. In time, this will stop because the copy machine will soon go the way of the landline telephone. The copying, legal and otherwise, will soon be done by Internet—no surprise here.

I'm grateful for readers and grateful for small pleasures. I possess no inner resources to convince others on this pitiful matter. This fall I will plant daffodils and tulips, possibly hyacinths, and will remember Oregon, a state with the loveliest spring colors. When the early bloomers appear, I will revel in the energy of their dormancy, asleep for months but now displaying their vibrancy. How splendid they stand in sunshine and wind. How unselfish those flowers that bloom briefly, like poets, offering images that remain after their fall.

TRYING TO WRITE A BEST SELLER

I BECOME AMBITIOUS when I consider best-selling authors, such as Stephen King, a writer of genuine talent, or Danielle Steel, a writer of slim talent but with legions of readers in all time zones. In truth, I'm bothered by the commercial successes of others. While Ms. Steel goes first class, champagne in her bejeweled hand, I, a poet, will go economy, peanuts spilling from the small bag I tear open with my teeth. I hunger for success, even a modest success. In my study—my bed, really, for that is where I work—my pencil scratches out ideas and lines of poetry on a yellow pad. The eraser scrubs the messy split infinitive and the unclear line. The paperback thesaurus has the last word.

At the moment I'm up late, the lamplight yellow with the theme of cowardice—no, that's not the word I'm after. I apply my turban-headed eraser to that infelicity. The scrubbings scramble onto the blanket. Like Poseidon, I blow them over the edge of the bed, then press a few crumbs to my thumb. Some of them stay pressed there, while others fall back onto the blanket. I ask myself: What do I know about cowardice? I pick up my pencil, dented with teeth marks, and then my dictionary, a workout in itself. Every short word belongs. Every long word, with two or three syllables, breaks belonging. I fan the dictionary, the five-hundred-plus pages creating a pleasant roar. This will be my fanfare, my wind of appreciation—how dreamy am I?

Wait a minute, I scold. I'm getting ahead of myself. I have only conjured up the word cowardice. I have produced nothing but eraser rubbings, some of which still lie on the bedspread while others have been blown like ants overboard. I nibble my pencil for mineral intake. I stroke my rabbit's foot for revival. I angle my reading light for inspiration—or at least perspiration, the moist clue that I have at least tried! I finally rub my forehead for its own oily dribble. As I say, I sometimes become ambitious, especially before sleep and the exit into a lovely dream. Not fifteen minutes into my best seller, the first word is already forgotten.

MY CAT WAS STARING AT an uncooked pinto bean on the kitchen floor. As I was alone with my failure to reach a reading public, I spoke to my cat. "Little buddy," I asked, "know what that is?" My buddy pawed the bean toward the stove. He licked his chops.

What genius for a creature with a brain the size of a pinto bean—he could see that the ancient seed must first be boiled! The cat washed his front paws with three licks.

"Little buddy," I confided, "I have an idea for a new poem. You want to hear it?" But before telling him, I held up a can of ocean-flavored cat food, in order to further deepen our man/cat relationship. I was introducing the can opener to him when a hummingbird suddenly hovered at the window—a braggart of a bird, bright as costume jewelry, his torso toylike, his beak laser thin.

The bird is all flash, I told myself, like some poets I know. He was gone before I could look him in the eye. Just me and my buddy again. When I opened the can, he pranced, the dinner bell on his collar ringing. My cat was born dressed in black, with a bib of napkin white on his chest. He would mix in nicely at the awards ceremony for the Nobel Prize for literature.

MY TIME WITH GEORGE W. BUSH

IN EARLY SUMMER 2001 I received a letter on behalf of Laura Bush, asking if I would participate in the first National Book Festival. I contemplated the letter, crisp as a priest's collar. I turned it over several times—a letter from the White House? A youthful friend, Mickey, had said that Laura Bush looked like the Joker from Batman. Was this really from the Joker? I grew scared, as if suddenly my phone was bugged. Was the FBI listening as I gulped a lozenge of fear? I trod down the stairs to our second-level bedroom. If I declined, would the IRS suddenly appear at my door? Would my name be placed on some list? I alerted my wife in her sewing room, "Carolyn, I think we're in trouble." I held out the invitation for her to see.

I meant that a decision had to be made, one that could seemingly place me in the wrong camp—we're Democrats and loathe the Republican Party. Other serious poets had, perhaps, received formal invitations as well, and more than a few, I was certain, were crumpling these letters and booting them into the fireplace. Should I accept? I e-mailed my friend Sandra Cisneros and, like a june bug, she seethed at the notion of attending. I wrote another poet and, no, he wasn't going—he had an anti-Bush sticker on his car bumper. Plus, he hadn't been invited. He was angry at not having a chance to scream NO.

I wrote Chris Buckley, editor and amigo, for advice. He told me to go! Eat and drink at the nation's expense, he argued, and make connections. Rub elbows! Shake hands! If I needed one, he could lend me a tweed jacket with elbow patches—a nice touch.

At that point in my career (and many other points, like right now), my poetry wasn't getting any attention—at least not on the East Coast. I could make use of this moment. Also, Chronicle Books, my poetry publisher at the time, agreed to front the airfare, provided that I pick up the hotel. That seemed equitable.

My wife and I rode Southwest Airlines, peanuts all the way, plus two beers purchased with drink coupons. We checked into a hotel (which will go nameless), had dinner on our own the first night and, the next day, after several hours of sightseeing, groomed ourselves for an evening with generals, ambassadors, politicians, scholars, intellectual librarians, festival sponsors, and rank-and-file writers, almost all of whom were relics and ready for the taxidermist. Did any of these writers share the same trepidations? Where were the other poets?

Earlier I had encountered Walter Mosley, a detective writer I admire, as we waited for a tour of the Library of Congress. Leaning against a column outside the library, Mr. Mosley was sage. I confessed my fears. He shrugged, said something to the effect that we writers were allotted one weekend to shine in the nation's capitol—why not accept these forty-eight hours? After we left, the city would once again dim.

I recall the evening, September 7. All of us had to go through portable metal detectors before stepping into the great halls of the Library of Congress. We moved at a nice pace, with novelist Gail Tsukiyama and her elderly mother at our side. Like Carolyn and me, Gail and her mother were from the Bay Area. Carolyn, a sansei, asked Gail about her family—what camp they were in during World War II, for instance. Gail and I talked a little literary shop, but not much. We kept looking around, trying to get our bearings. We were both newbies to this sort of occasion.

And where were we headed? Toward the Coolidge Auditorium where, before dinner, we would be treated to ten-minute lectures from well-known figures, including television anchor Tom Brokaw, novelist Gail Godwin, and historian David McCullough. We waited in plush chairs for President Bush and Laura Bush to appear. Music may have played, but I'm not sure. There was whispered chitchat among the seated, and the sound of fanning programs, a noise like bees, I thought, bees in a hive. Finally they did appear from the wings, George giving his well-known half-salute and Laura smiling like the Joker. We all rose to our feet; many applauded. I took my cue from Carolyn: keep your hands at your sides.

I sized up the six presenters, all distinguished in dress, all smart, all clear in their delivery, all courteous of each other's allotted time—perhaps this is why no poets were invited on stage, as we would hog the mics and look for offensive ditties to read. (We're often drunk and mad because the jumper cables we thought were in the trunk were not in the trunk. That's why we were late. Shit, shit, shit.) The applause that evening for the stellar six was sincere. I was moved by this brain trust. Our country was super smart.

We shuffled out of the auditorium in fair order, as most of the audience was elderly or, if not elderly, then civil. We all recognized an occasion and displayed good manners. We budged slowly over the carpet to an upper floor, where a candlelight dinner awaited. We stood in clumps and broke apart into smaller clumps. Soon Carolyn and I were escorted by a full-dressed Marine to our table, with glittery centerpieces, starched napkins, and cutlery shiny as trophies. A musical ensemble called the U.S. Army's Strolling Strings moved at a leaden pace through the large room. There was no need to be speedy, for the evening would be long.

Carolyn and I were seated with generals and with generals' wives in gowns. I stood up and peeked around: Condoleezza Rice was in a far corner, and Colin Powell sat by a large potted plant. And was that Donald Rumsfeld flanking the president's table? Even behind the glinting specs, the Washington types looked alike. How many in the room remembered that, in the 1980s, Rumsfeld had hugged Saddam Hussein in political glee?

And what was on the menu? Fish the size and thickness of a rich man's wallet, with a salad and veggies, and the typical buns that we craned onto our plates with silver tongs—so civil. The wines were white and the talk around the table not nearly as bright as the Strolling Strings. The generals' wives were indifferent to me, a poet, and were certainly not gaga over my wife's dress and jewelry, which was lovely, albeit not costly. I thought Carolyn's attire was understated and delightful, like the ice cream for dessert.

The president had been expected to greet each table, but work called him away. So we ate, drank, chatted, and after another hour we all left, the candle lights still shining. Carolyn and I returned to our hotel by taxi. The next day, on California time, we rose sleepily, showered, and dressed. Then we visited the White House—more metal detectors, more soldiers and security—where the writers (and a skinny poet) got to enjoy a buffet breakfast.

I was lifting little sausages onto my plate when the president came into the room. Out of respect, I lowered the sausages back down. His eyes, I recall, were puffy, as if he'd been crying. In truth, he was tired and among writers, a suspicious group. He stood straight, with his arms at his sides. He made no general remarks about the First Lady's efforts for the reading public, smiled thinly, then descended a small platform to speak, not to the writers, Laura's honored guests, but to a squad of NBA basketball players. What these towering athletes were doing with slouch-shouldered writers was anyone's guess.

After breakfast, Carolyn and I checked out of our hotel. The book festival, held on the grounds outside the Library of Congress, was in full swing. There were tents, vendors, and the buying public in the shape of families, lots of families, all very nice.

I had to leave Carolyn for an hour. A book signing beckoned! And once again, arms at my sides, I
walked through the metal detector posted at the
doors of the Library of Congress. We writers (eight
per hour) were each assigned a desk the size of a card
table. When the book buyers were let in, they too
had to go through the metal detector, a precaution
necessary because Laura Bush was in attendance.

When I saw my assigned desk, I immediately understood that something was wrong. Chronicle Books,
my publisher, hadn't shipped any books for sale, nor
had they asked a local bookstore to carry my titles
for the festival. I looked over at David McCullough,
whose biography of John Adams had been released
to spectacular reviews and robust sales earlier in the
year. The great man—Mr. McCullough, not President
Adams—was doing brisk business. There was a sales-
clerk at his desk, stacks of books, and a line that sometimes thinned but never petered out. I had nothing
to do except exercise my thumb by clicking my pen
open, then closed. A child came by, looked at me, and
walked away. I was, like, boring.

My chance for book sales was lost! I brooded at the
desk for an hour, my allotted time. Why would my
publisher strand me that way? I exited to find Carolyn
near a tent, where a reading by a novelist (I forget
who) was taking place. My wife was in the shade, with

our luggage at her side and a single purchase in hand: a Gail Godwin novel in paperback.

We had plans to fly back to California after my reading—ten minutes for the poet to make an appearance and leave listeners with a good impression. The stage was under a large tent, in the open, in other words, not the stately silence of Coolidge Auditorium. Flies pestered me before I even got on.

I was introduced by a very nice person in a visor-like hat. I read three funny poems in less than ten minutes and hustled off the stage, not pleased with my performance. I don't appreciate reading before an audience eating hotdogs. They were also drinking, fanning themselves with programs, and half listening, which isn't too bad, really—half listening is the best poets expect.

We flew home in the early evening, the pink horizon like a small inflamed wound. The next couple of days we watered our garden, did chores, answered mail, answered calls from our message machine, did errands, etc. We lived like any other couple and even argued about small matters, like dirty dishes in the sink. Then, two days after our return, two jetliners plowed into the Twin Towers. Another plowed into the ground in Pennsylvania. The Pentagon was harmed. Immediately, all air travel stopped. Days earlier the nation's capitol had been celebrating books and reading. Now devastation and smoke was stinging eyes.

The novelist Gail Tsukiyama and her mother had planned to stay after the festival to sightsee. The museums, however, were all shut down. Restaurants closed. Theaters dimmed their lights. Flights were cancelled. Numb, the nation huddled around television and computer screens. How or when our two Bay Area friends got home, I never found out.

EATS

WHILE FRESNO'S PALATE has recently become wide-ranging, dining in Fresno has not always been heralded as sophisticated. I'm thinking of 1983, when I drove 180 miles from Berkeley to Fresno to visit my buddy, poet Jon Veinberg. We needed to talk about the super 8 movie I was planning about a rock group called the *Ministers of Love*. In short, I was seeking to make a comedy, a sort of *Spinal Tap* without the music.

I arrived in the late afternoon. Jon and I drank beers in front of the television. Toward dusk, we left the house for a Basque restaurant, Yturri. Since it was a weekday, business was off. There was a young couple seated along the wall and two families with their elbows on the table, waiting for the second of five courses. Flies circled between the two major dining rooms, indecisive about which room to pester with their filthy buzz.

The waitress hurried over to us, plucked two menus from the side of the cash register, and led us to a table along the wall. We sat. We took a cursory peek at the menu, although we both knew we were going for deep-fried chicken. You couldn't beat the price: six-fifty for a five-course meal, with coffee and a choice of three kinds of ice cream to chase it all down.

We gave the waitress our order. Soon lentil soup was set in front of us, our spoons slashing like the paddles of rowboats. We next scraped two kinds of salad onto our plates: vinegary lettuce and potato with pimento. After that, chunks of stew, green beans, garbanzos. We tore pieces of French bread, which we buttered entirely yellow. We talked with food in our mouths, hungry as campesinos.

We raised industrial-strength wineglasses, dabbed at the corners of our mouths, and sighed for the good life. When the chicken came, piled on a plate, I waved mine off and asked the waitress to bring a doggie bag. She remarked, "Big boys can't do it?"

Jon patted his stomach, fully content. This is Basque eating: you eat most of what's presented on the large platters, then take the bird home.

We were gossiping about friends over coffee when one family, all sporting Fresno State Bulldog sweat-shirts, began to make faces at another, skinnier family at the end of their long, picnic-like table. Basque sheep-herders, working the valley, will often break bread at such tables. I quickly assessed the problem: the skinny family had lit up after dinner. More scowls, more smoke building up in the air. The threat of violence was like static—my hair was nearly standing up.

Within minutes, we heard the sturdy steps of the biggest son from the Bulldog family. The young man approached the father of the skinny family and ripped the cigarette out of his mouth.

"What the hell?" the father shouted. He got up half-way, eyes stoked.

Snickering, the bulldog son returned to his place at the table. His own father feigned innocence, while his mother turned to a daughter and muttered, "There's a 'No Smoking' sign right above his gourd. I swear!"

I was happy to hear that Fresno restaurants had become nonsmoking establishments, but this type of enforcement was like a Western movie, clumsy at best. Was a shoot-out next?

"You better watch it, Bulldogs," the father of the skinnies threatened, jabbing an angry finger into the air. His face was pink and excited. "You hear me?" He stood glaring while his own family—wife, two grown daughters, and a high school son—played with their dessert spoons, eyes down, embarrassed. Finally, the father sat down and picked up his fork.

Jon wagged his head. "I've been telling you for years, Gary. Fresno's crazy."

Both families began to mutter and throw ugly glances at each other. Finally, the waitress asked the Bulldog family what was the beef. Pointing fingers sprang up like spears, followed by accusations and more pink faces. The waitress listened like a schoolteacher, then disappeared into the kitchen and returned with two liters of house wine—one for each family. She poured the wine into tumblers.

With that, Jon and I, poets with our bagged chickens, set ten dollars each on the table and got out of the restaurant. No telling what would happen when anger was stoked by free alcohol.

A POSSIBLE GRANT FROM A FOUNDATION THAT WILL REMAIN ANONYMOUS, AS I MYSELF MIGHT APPLY

A FELLOW POET LAMENTS:

I've withered! I'm a tree with diseased sap running from wounds in its scabby bark. No honors have been bestowed upon me. I have an MFA, debt, and no job except one class teaching comp at a community college. I once came in third place in a literary contest no one has ever heard of—is this good enough for my résumé? Another time I read behind a famous poet and afterward lent the famous poet five dollars to get home on BART. Then a letter requested me to appear for a second-round interview for a $12,500 grant.

I dressed in what I thought was a clean shirt and ironed Dockers and left after double-locking my doors. I took a folder that contained nine new poems, in case the interview committee should ask. I rode BART and arrived with a human smell about me: BART stinks of joblessness. Obama should ride with us to his desk job at the Oval Office.

I inhaled, exhaled. I chewed gum until most of the flavor was gone and then spat that wad into a Kleenex. With the Kleenex, I wiped my brow—worry is such a workout. I spun myself through the revolving door of a tall building, which, if it were human, would be wholly vegan: it was so trim, not a tapeworm in its bowels.

I sat in a chair, legs crossed and then uncrossed. I waited with my hourglass going. I glanced at my poems—two typos in one, but the others were clean. Finally, a nice secretary in a dark business suit called my name. I rose with my folder of poems and told myself, Don't fuck up. Men with ends of their eyeglasses in their mouths sat behind a glass table when I entered. I beamed, so eager for a grant.

"Hi," I said. Thirteen floors up, the sound of "hi" is much thinner than when delivered at ground level. Smiling, I tried to push all the light inside me into my eyes. The eyes will tell someone whether you're worth the trouble. I sat down, scooting my chair and getting comfy. Shine, I told my inner being. Make an impression, for God's sake!

I was asked about my last fellowship. What was my last distinction? Where do I see myself in five years? The person who had asked the question was gripping my one-page vitae.

Last fellowship, last distinction, I thought, my thumbnail presenting itself to my mouth for a thoughtful chew. They were referring, of course, to a fellowship for writing, a genius grant (as in the MacArthur), an honor from an academy of arts and letters, a mortarboard and sash as recipient of an honorary doctorate from a Midwest college no one's ever heard of. And where would I be in five years? A poet attached to a wagon train of the homeless if money didn't come in— and quick!

"Well," I began meekly. "I get letters from kids in juvenile hall." I swallowed as I pictured a row of kids in orange suits sitting in orange chairs listening to me read poetry. "He's hella boring," I heard in my mind. I scratched egg from my white sleeve and imagined the sleeve as a priest's collar—just snip off the cuff and work it around my skinny neck. "But I don't have any, like, honors." There it was, in plain sight, my undecorated life. I had been runner-up for prizes that no one had heard of, but I kept that bit of truth harbored in my heart. I could have wept, thus extinguishing the light in my eyes.

They weren't pleased. Couldn't they see that I had written lots of books, some bestowing great personal honor, because I gave them my best? Didn't hard work count?

"You received a certificate for attending a writers' workshop," one remarked, looking down at my résumé. He was trying to help. "And it says here that you were a finalist for a prize from the California Arts Foundation." He looked up. Was there more about me than those two almost-made-it literary laurels? He waited.

But my brain couldn't ignite with a response. I was sinking through my chair; I was nothing but vapor! Didn't they know that it takes a lot to write poems that come in second?

I was out the door in ten minutes, the egg no longer on my sleeve but underneath my fingernails. I took the elevator down and tried to convince myself that, although my answer about the direction of my career had certainly stalled like a turtle, unlike a turtle I could change directions on a dime, and even trot.

On the street, cars honked while litter in the shape of burger wrappers lifted like ghosts. The pigeons, I noticed pathetically, were carrying away their own grants—French fries spilled on the sidewalk. A car turned the corner and frightened them. The birds fluttered into the air—no olive branches in their beaks. No, they were carrying fries home to their honeys. So where was my grant?

HOME ALONE

THE MOON WAS IN THE TREES, lighting up dead nests, and I had nothing to do but walk my pastoral block with my hands in my pockets, or sometimes hanging at my sides. There was nothing for my pleasure but well-kept lawns and old people in windows. I returned home to the porch light's cool glare. I unlocked my door and entered. There he was, my cat of thirteen years, which in human life is something like seventy-five years. He didn't bother to look up. His indifference said, "It's only him." When I called his name, this striped fellow, convict in pajamas, got up and trotted away. Framed against the picture window, he offered me a yawn before disappearing behind the couch, a leaf hitched like a flag on his tail.

I have never been charismatic. I have never influenced a living thing or a dead one. A first-book poet once asked, "Will you blurb my book?"

"No," I answered with sorrowful guilt. In my heart, I summoned up the past results of such requests: if my name appeared on the back cover, his book would sink like stone. "Will you write me a recommendation letter for a grant?" a Hmong poet pleaded. I replied, again with a chicken bone of guilt in my throat, "I've never gotten one of those grants you're seeking. Why would the fools listen to me?"

That night I slept face down, first on my left cheek, then my right, as if I were being slapped through seven hours of sleep. I got up with a wrinkle across my face, took a shower, and looked in the bathroom mirror. The wrinkle had not shaken out.

I drew open the kitchen's bamboo blinds. A passing neighbor, a relic, was using ski poles to balance his steps. When did this come into fashion? I watched him pass. Were the snows of death not far behind? Then the phone rang—Becky of Cardholder Services, asking if I would answer a three-question survey. The phone rang again—no one I recognized or could call a friend.

As it was morning, I walked around the block, just to readjust my bones and lube the pumps inside me. I returned home and browsed my bookshelf. I pulled out a book of poems by fellow poet Jon Veinberg, a book titled *An Owl's Landscape*, that may or may not have received any reviews. Published twenty-five years ago, I was aware of its strength then and I'm aware of it now. I read "Stretchmark Café," "Stray Dogs in the Rain," and "Sparrows as Ghosts." Each poem in that collection should have been made into posters and slapped onto college-dorm walls. Was it too late to tell Veinberg that I would be envious of this collection if I hadn't learned from these poems—maybe even swiped from them? I admire many lines, these particularly:

> Why do they shake their fingers at me—
> those dead clocks
> full of mysterious nods?

Mysterious nods—is that what time is, little nods at our movements, our deceits, our platters of chicken, our days, in other words?

I placed Veinberg's book back on the shelf, then was alerted by the red blink on the message machine. Becky of Cardholder Services again. I found myself in the kitchen and looked out the window, my eyebrows the eyebrows of an owl. Was I now among those old people with their faces in the window? I noticed two sparrows at the window box—Veinberg and me of the bird world?

Cheese sandwich for lunch, a small beer before dinner, then dinner in the shape of two turkey sandwiches. At sixty, my teeth were in my head, not in a jam jar on a nightstand—not bad. My hair, however, had made its escape. Was I ready for ski poles? What's it like to die with a spoonful of alphabet soup rising to your mouth?

I sighed for Veinberg, and for other poet friends: Buckley, Young, and Espada. Why do we do this to ourselves? We chirp to the world and no one visits our nests.

I assessed my accomplishments during the past twenty-four hours. The best thing I had done that day was peel an apple in one go-round, the peel like a scroll in my hands. I sat in my recliner and drank a beer, my fingers plying the label off the bottle, a habit of mine that I intend to break. With my wife gone, no one was calling, and no one was intending to call.

At that, I went off and wrote a poem.

THE END OF A COURTSHIP

I WAS IN A FRIEND'S BACKYARD drinking beer, telling yarns that stretched the truth like taffy, and listening to tales spun by others, the most tender regarding a doctor and his courtship of a woman who is now his wife. The doctor was smitten. Because he was in med school and broke (he is still broke, because he doctors the poor), he took her camping at Bass Lake, fifty miles north of Fresno. They slept side by side in sleeping bags and counted shooting stars. They watched the Big Dipper move across the heavens. In the morning, he took a shovel, then her arm, and led her to a private area where she could do her business.

The wife picked up the narrative, as she couldn't contain her laughter. "Marc would dig a hole and disappear, so I could use the toilet facilities." She was in love too. What man had ever treated her so kindly?

Relieving oneself in nature, among bees, jays, and the natural movement of wind through Manzanita and wildflowers . . . I could picture a hole, the dirt pale and then dark with urine, the hole filled and patted by the backside of a shovel.

After their third camping trip, the pair woke to sunlight bright as a scalpel. "It was a lovely day," the doctor's wife exclaimed, before continuing. "But I knew the courtship period was over when Marc handed me the shovel. From then on, I had to dig my own hole."

My eyes shut from laughter. Behind my eyelids, I saw wildflowers of many colors sprouting where she had squatted in dust, in love.

A WOMAN STOPS HER CAR

WHEN I WAS SEVENTEEN, I sent a tomato through our kitchen window. I had been playing war with a younger brother and the garden tomato was a grenade. The glass lay in the driveway, with shards gleaming on a small bush like Christmas ornaments. Fear buzzed through my body. I would be in trouble with my parents. My mother would snort steam, her anger like a hot iron, and my stepfather would mutter from his recliner, booze leaking from his eyes.

I had been waiting to escape for a long time. The thought of running away had rumbled through my mind a month earlier. The moment was upon me—the tomato, stuck on the wall, was like my heart, its wet interior leaking downward.

I went inside the house, grabbed a paper bag, and filled it with socks, a change of underwear, a comb, and candy. I walked up Tulare Street toward downtown and crossed the tracks. From there I took a Greyhound bus. Six hours later I was in Los Angeles, then, after I pushed my thumb out, Santa Monica.

I was a runaway. It was July 1969, the year we sent a man to the moon, and the year I rediscovered the ocean, at least for a day. In Santa Monica I trod through the heavy sands of the public beach. It was late afternoon. The lowering sun was still shiny as a hurt eye. I sat on the beach and lay with my hands on my chest, eyes closed. I pictured my parents, the two of them, then my mother, singularly. She would have come home from wherever she had gone that morning, made an furious face at the tomato stain on the wall, asked angrily about me, searched for a belt, gotten even angrier when I didn't show for dinner. Then, softening, she would have looked out the window. Where is Gary? Where is my son?

Darkness came and I wasn't home.

I was in Southern California, amazed at the progress of my actions, suddenly alone among sunbathers, a multitude I didn't know—lovers, teenagers, families, roaming surfers, would-be gang members. I approached the ocean, the roar growing in my ears. The waves lapped my ankles, but I didn't risk the rolling surf. Kites were being yanked about in a strong ocean breeze.

I pushed my thumb out again. The next thing I knew I was in a place called Burbank. I was hungry and thirsty. That first night, I broke into a church and devoured a box of crackers from a cupboard. I slept in a pew, rose early, and went walking down Mission Boulevard. I had about three dollars in bills and change. At a coffee shop I bought a stack of pancakes and ate every bit, my fork dripping with syrup like glue. I licked it clean.

The second night, I slept in a car. The third night, I slept in another car. I survived on corn nuts and breath mints, stuff found in the glove compartments. By day four, I had found a job at Mission Tire Factory and would work there, in its inferno, for six weeks, piling up 134 dollars, the most money I'd ever had—and it was mine. The money would be for school, or for the broken window if necessary. Imagining my mother and stepfather, framed by the window, picture-perfect, I'd had the urge to hurl another tomato at it.

This was a time of hippie love, when drivers were willing to pick up hitchhikers from the side of the road. My hair was short, and I was clean at the start of the day. What risk was there in stopping for a boy with a lunch bag in his hand?

But the work in the factory made me black by the end of the day. It was a six-mile trek back to my rented room. No one gave me a ride, though I still carried the lunch bag, now empty. Could I blame them? I was dirty with soot. When I got to my new home, I would have to hose myself off, clothes and all. This quick wash took place on the backyard lawn. I would strip off my wet socks and shirt, then sit in the sun until I was almost dry before going inside and laying down on my bed, exhausted.

While I was walking home one afternoon, a Mexican woman stopped her car. She came toward me with a dollar bill and said, in accented English, "Take it." The woman's sudden appearance surprised me. I raised my hand to fend off the money. She begged me to take it, but I told her no, that I was OK, that I was close to home. (Home. Where was that place?) She was concerned for me and her concern, I believe, rose from having lived through rough times herself. I refused her once again, this woman, who was now frantic. She demanded that I take it, and I insisted that I was OK, that I was just dirty, not penniless. Finally, she returned to her car, which was parked on the other side of the road, and drove away.

This was over forty years ago. I've made mistakes in my life and this is one of them. I should have accepted that dollar, which would have demonstrated her charity. She was trying to help; she was showing me tenderness. I was a son walking away, my clothes and body darker than the shadow at my side.

SMALL CONJECTURES

I'M IN MY MOTHER-IN-LAW'S rural yard, within earshot of a neighbor's tractor and its miraculous blades pulling off ears of corn. The evening is blood-red on a line of grapevines. A breeze whips the pale flags of dish towels on the clothesline. Nelson, the dog, rattles his chain. The first headlights sweep out front, but nothing is gathered up. I get up from the lawn chair and walk to the barn, latched with a rusty spike. I undo the spike. When I throw open the door, the heat of the day heaves toward me and wraps me in a bear hug. I tug at the front of my sweaty shirt as I walk into the barn. A busted tractor and an altar of oil drums catch my eye. I touch a gas-pump handle—this is a small family farm with its own supply in a tank in the ground. When I churn the handle, an exhaust of panting ghosts rises from below.

I return to the lawn chair. My memory for happiness flounders like a fish. My friend Ernesto Trejo is dead and two of my three friends are mad at me— what did I say? I wish I could start the decade over by being nicer.

But not all is lost. There's my wife gathering those dish towels from the line. She's on tiptoes—she's short but casts a long shadow in my life. The sun has dropped, the whole west pink as a fresh, puckered wound.

"Hey, girl," I call to my wife. There's a clothespin in her mouth. She puts it back on the clothesline and doesn't bother to turn her head.

I call my wife again, then once more. She finally comes over and sits on my lap, the pile of dish towels pressed to her breasts. I part the towels, unbutton the top button of her Hawaiian shirt, with the hula girl print, and look in. Those breasts will replace the two good friends I lost. Like Santa, I ask, "Have you been a good girl?" She squirms off my lap and slaps me with a dish towel. Is this what they mean by a dominatrix? She returns to the house, where the refrigerator is humming to keep things cold. The cooler in the window can't spin fast enough to stop our faces crying with sweat. Who invented summer?

My mother-in-law's house is in the country, west of Fresno. It's almost dark, and it's almost time for a beer to come out of the freezer. The ice cubes have melted in my iced tea. I spill the dilution at my feet.

Now why are my friends mad at me? I'm pondering this question when the screen door slaps open and my wife appears, profiled darkly against the porch light. She comes down the cement steps toward me. She's barefoot, I see, with a hand on the top button of her shirt. I stand up to greet her, mud dimpled on my toes from the splash of iced tea.

We do it behind the barn, like two teenagers, the moon above and a more beautiful one right in front of me.

DON'T DO IT

IN 1921 ENGLAND the master of a public school was lecturing youth, ages ten to fourteen, on the consequences of masturbation—such as the growth of hair on their palms and, even more serious, the blindness—if they didn't stop. The master said, in so many words, that the faculty could smell masturbation down the hallway. It stunk. It stained sheets and fouled underwear. It was against God's wishes.

All the youth blinked at the master and his fellow teachers. The master reiterated: blindness—who would want to be blind and miss the beauty of the world?

A few chairs scraped against the floor, a door somewhere opened and shut; farther away, a train whistled. Other than these sounds, the hall was quiet until one young man stood up, his school tie crooked, his hair tousled as if just from bed. "Sir," he bravely asked, "can we do it just until we're farsighted?"

Snarky tyke, Cambridge-bound, and a poet in the making.

BILINGUAL LOVING MAKING

SAMUEL PEPYS, civil servant and memoirist, was a rogue outside the marriage bed. His first wife was Elizabeth, and their servant girl/companion in the year 1667 was Deborah Willet, or Deb, just out of her teens. Pepys, age thirty-three, was smitten with Deb. He enjoyed her youthful beauty, her ability to play cards, and her flirty presence when they traveled. In love, he became bilingual—his engorged member demanded that he speak in Spanish and English— Spanglish. In his diary, he wrote after scolding Deb for poor grammar, "I did give her good advice and beso la [kissed her], ella weeping still; and yo did take her, the first time in my life, sobre mi genu [on his knees] and poner mi mano sub her jupes and toca su thigh . . ." Later, when Deb left the household (Elizabeth had put her foot down), Pepys frowned, heartbroken at the loss of his plaything. He tracked her down days later and perfumed the air with romantic stuff. He wrote in his diary after an excursion in his coach to what we might call Lover's Lane, "tener mi cosa [his dick] in her mano, while mi mano was sobra su pectus [a little Latin thrown in] and so did hazer [sic] with grand delight."

But Elizabeth found out about Pepys's excursions. Had she spies? Another servant who tattled? Elizabeth screamed as most sensible wives would scream. She forbade his leaving the house unless chaperoned by their mutual friend, Will Hewer. Repentant, Pepys agreed to her terms and, to cement these terms, he made love to his wife, then fell on his knees to pray to God for guidance and such. When he rose to his feet, he saw that the upholsterers had finished redoing their bedroom. That put him in a good mood, such finery in a troubled time of marriage. He didn't speak bilingually again for a good many years.

WHILE MY POET FRIEND didn't have a horse-drawn coach to park on Lover's Lane, he did get.involved in a tangled affair. It began in a car with 140 horses under the hood. They had smooched, he told me, and felt each other out on a bench before he directed her to the car. My friend did that "tener mi cosa" thing. Their breath thickened the air and heavy petting led to zippers being undone and a sports bra peeled off. With flesh on flesh, the car squeaked and owls hooted in nearby trees. It would have been a good night except my friend's wife found out a day later. She raged like the angriest fire. She asked, "How many times did you do it?" The shivering poet—non-bilingual and lost for words—stuttered, "Once. And it was hardly in there very long."

Graphic detail never helps.

PARTY TALK

"I DON'T OWN A CELL PHONE. Never have," I remarked, holding sour cream dip on the end of a celery stalk. I was prepared for conversation on this matter. And it came.

"Like, what?" a young woman asked in astonishment. "What if people want to, like, talk?" She made this remark while rolling up her sleeves—revealing tattoos of varying colors and ambiguous design.

I waved my celery stick like a conductor's wand. In answering the inquisitive young lady, I said that I could be reached at home, or people could talk to me when they saw me.

She asked, "What if you're in the airport and, like, your flight is late?"

Nibbling on the celery, I answered: "Oh, I just wait until I get home to tell my wife that the flight was, like, late." The dip was tart.

"How about if you're in an accident?" she countered. She took a sip of white wine, then muttered, "Oh, damn," when her contact lens floated out of position. She set her wineglass down. She bowed her head and began to readjust the contact lens, her fingers peeling her eyelid very wide.

Because I thought she was still listening, I answered: "Like, it wouldn't matter, because I'd probably be, like, dead. Or if not dead, then, wow, in some serious pain. A jet going down is serious shit."

"What?"

She hadn't been listening. Her head was now raised, the contact lens in place. I remained quiet until her vision cleared and she could once again concentrate on this conversation, which had an intensity equal to that of putting on a pair of clean socks. She remarked, none too quietly, "This party is boring. I wonder if I'll get a job."

I couldn't argue the point; it was a professional gathering of librarians in late afternoon. Even the festive balloons were crawling down the wall.

I disengaged myself from the young woman, but thought of her as I sneaked back to the buffet table where, with ginger fingers, I craned broccoli, cherry tomatoes, and carrot sticks onto my plate. I'll be dead by the time she's my age, I thought, as I poured dip onto my plate. I'll have drunk what there is to drink. I'll have eaten what there is to eat, and I'll have listened to too much chitchat. I'll be the dust that makes you sneeze when the conversation at such gatherings is repeated.

What's required, at my age, is an hourglass to turn over, to let the sands hiss one more time.

THE FEAR OF MATH

IN 1989 I WAS WORKING ON a poem that included a math equation, which admittedly was beyond me, like a star or the black hole behind the star. Our daughter, the mathematician in the house, was only in fourth grade. She knew only so much. I needed an equation higher than her step stool, so decided to pester Professor Singh across the street. He mowed the lawn, he washed his car, he fathered children. A regular guy, he would appreciate my effort to expand my horizons. In his doorway, I told him what I needed—a high school math problem to fill a junction in a funny poem that legions of readers would giggle over. He blinked behind his thick lenses when I handed him a yellow tablet.

He wrote out:

$$x = \frac{-b \pm \sqrt{b^2 - 4ac}}{2a}$$

It took him all of eight seconds to write it. I looked at my yellow tablet, my donkey hooves shuffling beneath me. What did it mean? I didn't even begin to get it, so I complained: "No, no, something more like junior high."

Professor Singh looked at me in wonder. His eyes grew stern. He said, "My friend, this is junior high."

FABLE OF THE LOST POETS

MOTHERS DRAIN a public pool and don't find their poet sons at the bottom. They part a neighbor's bush as if looking for a shuttlecock—no sons there. They speak to a stray dog, the last traveling monk with holy beads of water hanging from his chops. They holler in a sycamore tree: "Are you up there, smarty-pants?" On their knees, they look under beds, turn those shirts on the floor inside out. With hands over their mouths, they slowly open the trunk of the car in the yard: no smothered bodies, no cord around a blue throat, no blood-flecked wristwatch with time hustling ahead.

If they're going to write, poets must abandon family. They must step into cold rivers—no footprints pressed in sand, no ripped shirttail snagged on a branch, no smoldering cigarette at the edge of the bank, no clues to say that their demise was criminal. Poets must appreciate their surroundings—the moon is grinding its way west, in full daylight, and the interiors of clouds are sharpening their knives. Some god has ordered lightning to strike, winds to shake a dead rabbit's satchel of bones.

At a levee, the poets pour sand through their fingers and use up time. "I can't wait to get out of here," one child poet complains, because last night at dinner family members fought over the largest drumstick. There was yelling and drunkenness at this table, a singular incident in which a glass of milk was overturned and a spanking followed.

Mothers search. Fathers get into trucks and look too. But the poet is gone, soundless as smoke, with eighty-four units toward a BA in English from a state college in the Midwest. The disappearance takes him from the city to the country of bullet-pierced stop signs, then to a new city. There he rents a room with a ladder and bookshelves all the way to the ceiling. If he climbs that ladder, if he tiptoes on the last rung, he will find his books at the very top, his books there, among many millions, but there all the same.

TROUBLEMAKER

I HAVEN'T BEEN TOO LOUD or controversial, though I'll smart off against the Republican Party at the drop of a sombrero. But in August 1997 trouble did visit me. I discovered that my picture book *Chato's Kitchen* had been placed on the restricted list in Clovis, California, once a cowboy town with real cowboys but now a vast expanse of subdivisions with names like Sunset Lakes and Pheasant Landing. Clovis rubs next to Fresno, but Chato and his *carnal* (sidekick), Novio Boy, rubbed Clovis the wrong way.

"Hmm," I said, when I got a call from a friend in Fresno. In his anger, he seemed a tangle of illogical rhetoric. He called Clovis racist, he called the town dumb, he called the residents of this haven of nice homes dummy racists. However, wearing a bathrobe cinched at the waist, I was Zen for the first time in my life.

What had happened? A single parent complained that the picture-book characters were too *cholo*, too gangster in appearance, with bandanas across their foreheads, studs in their ears, a Christian cross (sacrilege), and wifebeaters under Pendleton shirts. The guttersnipish dialogue—"Yo! Cool Cat of East Los, Homes"—was not appropriate. Plus, Novio Boy was partially attired in red, the gang color of Fresno's "Bulldogs." (A bulldog is also the mascot of Fresno State, with the football and basketball teams having their own problems with the law.)

In the book's narrative, Chato, a suave, streetwise kitty, invites his newly arrived neighbors—a mouse family—over for dinner. But Chato has a hidden motive. He plans a sumptuous meal, with the mice (*papi* and *mami* mouse, plus the children) as the main course. The mouse family agrees to the neighborly gathering, provided they can invite a friend. Chato is thrilled at the thought of another mouse for the grill.

On the day of the party, Novio Boy rolls up his sleeves to help in the kitchen. The two cats busily prepare side dishes of arroz and frijoles, guacamole, pico de gallo, *horchata*—the works. When the hour of the party arrives, the home cats are surprised when the mouse family's friend, the extra guest, is a long wiener dog named Chorizo. That evening, the banquet is entirely vegetarian.

Once a book is placed on the restricted list, a parent has to provide a note before a child can read the book. But again, how did my book get on this list? Because a single parent complained. And following this complaint, a committee of parents, teachers, administrators, and law enforcement officials met, agreed to the first parent's viewpoint, and then assigned my two cats to the kennel. One librarian, Martha Rowland, petitioned that the book remain available to all. "I personally like the book," she said, "and have used it with students and they love it. What kids like about the book is the story; they don't focus on the clothes of the characters. This book isn't about gangs. It's about cats trying to catch mice for dinner." Later, in a *Fresno Bee* editorial—and after many letters about the Chato controversy—parent Patty Aoki wrote, "To me, the book is about the universal understanding that everyone is different and that we shouldn't be afraid of people because they're different."

"*Orale pues*," Chato would meow. "That's right."

In Spanish there's a word, *pedo*, which means "fart" but also means a stink over nothing. Thus, in the late summer of 1997, claims of censorship, even racism, were insinuated, and my name appeared in the *Fresno Bee*, on the front page even. Of course, the telephone rang off the hook. I made a few remarks to defend the book but they had no fire behind them. I could see that the Fresno community wanted all-out war, but I remained quiet as a mouse with cheese on my cracker, far from heated debate. I did appear on Radio Bilingue, for fifteen minutes of chatter with poet Juan Felipe Herrera, then professor of Chicano/Latino Studies at Fresno State. But even then I didn't shoot my mouth off. No, this was a new Gary, a Zen Gary, Life Coach Gary, a purpose-driven Gary, a sober-minded Gary.

The public was strongly in favor of releasing Chato and Novio Boy from the restricted list—racial profiling of these characters would not be tolerated. There were letters to the editor titled "Wrong Focus," "Sad Decision," "The Ban on 'Chato,'" "Learn Something," "Thanks for the Tip," and "Fearful Adults." Lessa Tyrell wrote, "This is in regard to the Aug. 1 article about Gary Soto's 'Chato's Kitchen.' I have been asking myself, 'What is wrong with this picture?' I am not talking about the pictures in the book of Chato and his compadre. I am talking about the racist picture Clovis Unified is creating by restricting this book. Why is it that the only two books Clovis has tried to ban lately have been written by minorities? The other is 'I Know Why the Caged Bird Sings' by Maya Angelou."

"You go, girl," Novio Boy would meow.

In November, after Martha Rowland's petition, the Clovis Unified School District held a meeting. They met in public, and two hundred parents, students, and activists came to rescue Chato and his *carnal*, Novio Boy, from an educational pound. You could see it coming: the restricted-list status was repealed and the book went back on the shelf. The editor of the *Fresno Bee* wrote "Hurray for Chato," a kindly appraisal of the district's reversal. They were brave and should be applauded.

As for me, I was Zen, in my Zen car, with Zen music echoing off my headliner. I have always known that no child who reads books, even a book like mine, has ever become a gang member.

INSOMNIA

THE PASTRY CHEF suffered insomnia when he was four, a little guy with his thumb in his mouth, unable to sleep. When asked, "What did you think about?" the pastry chef, forever sleepy-eyed, answered, "I thought about the past." Now an old man, he stirred his coffee, yawned, and remembered when he was three and a half, a warm time, when his bed had become an oven to his first years. "Oh, that was a good time," he reflected nostalgically, "when I was three years and two months old." He was already losing time then—little boy pliable as dough with his thumb in his mouth, a sweetness of life.

For poets the past is lamentable, the future fearful, until it too comes around and is placed softly in the past.

MY TIME WITH HAROLD BLOOM

I WAS BEHAVING MYSELF when poet Luis J. Rodriguez alerted me that Harold Bloom had uttered some unkind words about my poetry. I was surprised to be on the professor's critical radar. I was further surprised that Bloom's curtness toward me appeared in *Newsweek*—the October 10, 1994 issue, if you care to do your own digging. The article, written by David Gates and titled "It's Naughty! Haughty! It's Anti-Multi-Culti," updated for worrywarts the hijacking of culture by multicultural interests. The tone of the article implies this: that multicultural literature—and multicultural life, to boot—is corrupting our country; that we're getting dumber and dumber because of the diversity of literature taught in college classrooms. Gates first draws on popular books that speak of the despair common among serious and thoughtful people—the country is going to the dogs. He cities Dinesh D'Souza's *Illiberal Education*, Arthur M. Schlesinger's *The Disuniting of America*, and Robert Hughes's *Culture of Complaint*. He cites the late *Time* magazine writer William A. Henry III's *In Defense of Elitism*. Henry the third says, "The wrong side is winning." The social critic also says, "It is scarcely the same thing to put a man on the moon than to put a bone through the nose." O Jesus! I cried, suddenly blasphemous, then double Jesus, when I read that Henry had received awards for his efforts in civil rights. How has putting a man on the moon made the planet any better? I side with savages with bones in their noses any day.

Gates's article finally arrives at the subject of the week, namely Harold Bloom, Sterling Professor of Humanities at Yale (he also had a position at NYU at the time) and author of twenty books on literature, language, and culture. His new book was *The Western Canon*, five-hundred-plus pages which argue that "great" literature should return to the university classroom. Bloom further argues that multicultural lit has crowded the syllabi of even the most prestigious colleges—a shame. When asked which writers would be indispensable on a desert island, he frets over the question, but finally names Shakespeare, Cervantes, Milton, Dickens, Proust, and Kafka, plus the authors of the Bible.

All other writers, great and minor, read and unread, rich and poor, would have to dogpaddle to their own islands, or drown. I can't argue against all of the literary figures on Bloom's boat, but I'll go public here and say that most readers would need a handful of NoDoz to rouse interest in Milton. His poetry is a moralizing bore, long-winded, and simple in spite of his rhetoric. One function of literature is to entertain, and the bearded one, I'm afraid, is bedside reading only if you want eight hours of sleep.

I know that after this comment I'll be pigeonholed as a dumbed-down holder of a diploma from a barber college instead of Fresno State, which to most Ivy Leaguers is already no better than a GED. Alright, I eat Cheetos by the handful. I follow the recipes in *Better Homes and Gardens*. I like the Bee Gees and *Dumb and Dumber*, the movie. How dare Soto, a minor talent, proclaim Milton a yawner! Let's just remember that Soto's on the wrong side, after all.

Gates's article totters between agreeing and disagreeing with Bloom. Little snippets of language suggest that he is not entirely convinced by Bloom's argument. But enough of the article and more about me! In a sidebar interview with *Newsweek*'s Ken Schulman, we catch Bloom letting his hair down—the hair on the sides of his skull, at least. He answers questions like, "Does literature have a social function?"

"What does this 'school of resentment' resent?" "Who are these hypocrites?" "What will replace the canon?" This is where I, a poet, come in. Bloom cites a scholar and friend at the University of Chicago who says my poems are being used in her introductory course in literature. He remarks, after speaking of Hemingway and Chekhov, that "Gary Soto couldn't write his way out of a paper bag."

Once again I am reminded of my GED from Fresno State—no, I mean my certificate from Moler Barber College. Professor Bloom is one of our country's better-known scholars and, in spite of his degrees, both earned and honorary, he is not above anger. Here, as judged by his tone, he comes off as a scold. The fact that my work is read at the university level enrages him, because such poetry is responsible for the demise of learning. Why blame me? I'm just writing poetry, pushing a pencil with Cheeto stains. How am I responsible for the culture of stupidity?

Having taught at the university level, I'm familiar with the type: Professor Bloom belongs in the camp of academics who, when they don't get their way, will pout (indeed, *Newsweek* includes a photo of Bloom pouting as he feigns reading a book). Academics hold grudges. They vote against you in departmental meetings, just because. They walk past you if you don't agree with them on the smallest of literary matters. We should consider this: literature, like a great city, is not stagnant. If new writers surface, as they do, generation after generation, why blame them for the change in reading habits? For lowering the standards? For the breakdown of anything considered sacred? Literature, both great and minor, moves in trends. That it moved temporarily in my favor—and eventual disfavor, if this makes Professor Bloom happy—is not uncommon. While Hemingway and Steinbeck were giants in their time, both have lost their luster. Their work has become suspect. Bloom of all academics should be aware that what might be recognized as a good read at the moment may become in time, like Milton, a yawner. I've seen students yawn at my work. Since I'm alive, I yawn back at them. Snark, snark.

Gates's article was published in 1994. Was I hurt by Bloom's outburst? No. But it did give me cause for reflection. Why is it that the most humane people I've met are not scholars with abbreviations after their names? I have encountered farm workers with a deeper sense of courtesy than many academics; farm workers who are patient when listening to the other side, unlike the academics who argue against each other without ever learning from a different viewpoint. I've read histories in which peasants live their lives with serene determination (for example, *Dark and Bloody Ground* by F. Perez Lopez), while I've seldom met an academic who isn't angry about something uttered in a faculty committee meeting.

That I don't rank with Shakespeare and Proust, Cervantes and Dickens, or with many writers hailed as great in Bloom's Western Canon, I will acknowledge. But in my view, his unkindness represents not a blemish on my career, but a badge of honor. Fuck him.

COURTESY

DOLORES VELASCO, a former nun and friend of mine at the United Farm Workers, was once invited by a female farm worker to a house built of cardboard. This structure was located behind an abandoned barn and away from the road. It was early February, wet, the blossoms from any number of fruit trees blowing across the fields. Dolores couldn't say no and followed this woman, who had been on a picket line for several hours outside of McFarland, California. There, kneeling in the cardboard house, the farm worker took a glass bowl from a box. She peeled three oranges and parted them into wedges, which were then lightly peppered with cayenne and sprinkled with salt. She found a dishtowel to serve as a communal napkin. The bowl, a chalice of friendship, was set before them. They ate with their hands, Dolores told me, salt on the edges of her fingers.

What we can learn from such courtesy.

RIDES

SOMETIME IN THE MID-EIGHTIES I was invited to do a poetry reading at a college in Los Angeles. My book *Black Hair* has just come out to kind notices, including one trumpeting review in the *Christian Science Monitor*. I'm puffed up like a bird. I have this paying gig—five hundred dollars—and a chance to peddle my new book. A dollar off the list price, but hey, readers! I imagine thirty students in the audience. I then expand on this number. In my mind the audience grows to over a hundred—that's enough for my ambition. The introduction will be clumsy, the glass of water will be from a fountain in a hallway, and the podium will rock when I lean my elbows on it. I don't care! One person in the audience (massive mustache) will walk out because I'm not Chicano enough. But the rest will remain seated, including old professors leaking water from their eyes. They've been up since before dawn. They are obligated to remain on campus and hear me out.

I fly into LAX from Oakland. I wait at the curb as instructed by my host, a Chicano instructor I'd met a year ago at a party that lasted until a red dot of sun was visible in the east. He was the faculty advisor of MEChA, a statewide Chicano student organization. I do what I am told and stand at the curb looking left for a white van. There are a lot of such vans, including those from immigration—*la puta migra*! Each time a white van roars by I raise an arm, my way of saying, "It's me!" The drivers momentarily glance at me, indifferent to my little salute. Who in the world is that skinny fuck waving at me?

I step from the curb to the sidewalk and then back onto the curb, my way of keeping warm. I grow lonely, less self-confident, no longer one of the tribe of puffed-up poets.

Finally, a van with the fingerprints of hell on the windshield shimmies up to the curb. Smoke of burning oil refineries rolls from its exhaust.

Jesus, I think. Is this my ride? The front tires are bald. The headlights are cross-eyed. The antenna is a coat hanger.

"Hey, Gary!" my host calls from the window, his hand out and waving. He's happy to see me. He gets out and gives me an *abrazo*, a bear hug of friendship, and takes my small suitcase, heavy with books. He opens up the sliding door of the van, which confuses me. Shouldn't I get in the front?

I hoist myself into a dark cavern that smells of oily car parts. Immediately, I notice there is no place to sit other than the floor. I squat, and do my best to appear dignified, the hem of my newish jacket pulled up like a skirt. I then scoot my luggage under my butt—that's better. I notice a tiny woman with long braids sitting shotgun. I wait for her to turn and say hello. She doesn't, so I say, "Hi, I'm Gary," and with that she extends an arm. She asks, through the release of smoke, "Want some?"

"Some" is a lipped roach of power *mota*, marijuana.

I'm shaking my head no when my host hops into the van and says, looking up into the mirror, "We were circling above. This is Norma."

"Above" is departures; I had been "down" in arrivals. Norma nods her head at the windshield.

"No problem," I say and grip my suitcase. My host is not in the least embarrassed to be shuttling a poet in the back of his dirty van. The van moves in a lurch. Corn nuts slide from one side of the van to the other, like a hockey game, I think. Corn nuts and small white-and-red Legos.

"Bring books?" my host inquires. His eyes are in the mirror.

I pat my suitcase and yell, "Lots!"

The van picks up speed. Potato chip bags levitate from the wind that slices through the open windows. We take a few corners out of the airport and in minutes we're on the freeway. I can't see much from my dark hole and for a moment think: this is what it's like to be kidnapped. I can't hear because the music is cranked up, bad speakers playing a Santana classic.

My host's eyes return to the rearview mirror, and then the mirror fills with really big teeth. He's happy to have me at his college.

I nod my head.

He screams, "You're, like, awesome."

I nod my head. I can see that we're on the 405, right on the tail of a truck. The bumpers are almost kissing.

"You dig this music?" More teeth, more happiness from my host, as he takes the roach and inhales, sparks ticking off his face, then fading to nothing.

I'm now sliding like the corn nuts but holding on, for I have a new book out, an anticipated audience of one hundred, a review in a prestigious magazine, and five hundred dollars coming. Life is good, life is moving at a greater speed than ever. In my craziness I think that fame is like this, you gripping something familiar—such as your suitcase—and traveling down the 405 before rush hour.

I make it to the reading. No professors with leaky eyes but sixteen students, all brown as me, and my host still smiling his toothy smile. Norma is stroking first her left braid, then the right, then the left again. I read, then answer questions like, "How do you get published? My brother-in-law is working on poetry." I find out this brother-in-law is doing five to ten for armed robbery.

It's a good night. I party with some of the audience; get drunk from a large bottle of red wine; eat chips and salsa, canned bean dip, and a hotdog in a piece of bread. I sleep on the floor that night, a cadaver draped with a single blanket. The next morning I ride shotgun back to the airport, with most of my books returning with me.

My host drops me off at arrivals and pulls away, his large teeth in the side mirror. I never see fame or the five hundred dollars.

SOMETIME IN THE EARLY NINETIES I'm invited to the Dallas Children's Film Festival, because of my short film *The Pool Party*. I'm glad for the invitation, though in my heart I know that I'm a poet, not a film-maker. I accept the offer because Hayley Mills, the child actor of the early 1960s, will also be honored. In my youth I enjoyed all her films, especially the moody and atmospheric *The Chalk Garden*. Also honored will be an Academy Award winner for special effects, from Industrial Light & Magic (his name will not be mentioned).

I go. I mingle. I tell my inner self, Don't drink too much. Just sip. At the hotel reception, I stare at Hayley Mills, who is accompanied by a much younger man who resembles Hugh Grant—yummy, some women (and men) might muse. In her early fifties, Hayley Mills is attractive as well as pleasant. She's the center of the evening. She has style.

But style goes only so far. The conversation lags. There's laughter, canned laughter, from us all. We're thrown together and don't know each other. The minutes grind, drinks are brought to our faces, goodies grabbed from trays that appear over our shoulders.

I'm wishing to make a remark that will get Hayley Mills's attention, but witty words and insightful phrases refuse to issue from my mouth into the air. What could I possibly say to this star from the 1960s? "Hey, I write kick-ass poems. Want me to read you one?"

The Academy Award winner is a large and quiet man. He smiles, mouth closed, through his clipped beard. He holds a glass of sparkling water in both hands, as if it weighs a ton. This tame reception is being attended by board members of the Dallas Children's Film Festival, plus a few students from Southern Methodist University. Some, I will learn, are acting as gofers.

I continue to mingle. I resist a third glass of white wine. I talk with an uneaten cracker in my hand. Then it's time to head to dinner. I put down my cracker and rub my fingertips together, crumbs falling like snow to the carpeted floor. The organizer of the festival pulls me aside. "Gary," he says, "you're going to ride with Kirsten." He waits for my reaction, biting his lower lip.

"What?" I ask. The waitstaff has taken away my wine glass and my eyes follow its departure on a small silver tray.

"Kirsten is a volunteer," the organizer says. "You met her earlier." His tone is now almost somber.

I'm confused as I turn my full attention to the organizer, who is my height, younger, but already with gray wings of hair at his temples. I blink at him and then, as if through a thirty-five-millimeter camera, it all comes into focus. Kirsten, a student at SMU, will drive me to dinner, while Hayley Mills and the Academy Award winner ride in the limousine I saw parked outside. Oh, I get it.

The organizer hopes he hasn't hurt my feelings. He whispers, "It was in her contract."

I'm neither hurt nor bothered. Hayley Mills deserves the limo: she was a star and still is in my book. The Oscar winner for special effects? Him too! I touch the organizer's shoulder and tell him, "No problem."

I'm re-introduced to Kirsten, who is slapping her hands of cracker dust. She smiles, her face brightening naturally. We shake hands, the bangles on her wrist chiming a pretty little tune. She shoulders her purse. She leads me outside to a clunker of a two-seater Honda sitting alone in the parking lot.

"It's unlocked," she tells me. Her hurried footsteps are sharp against the asphalt.

I hop in. My knees are up to my chin—this Honda, from the late 1970s, is as small as an astronaut's capsule. On the dash are cassettes. I pick one of them up: Fleetwood Mac. I set it back down.

"Sorry about my car," Kirsten says as she buckles up, her own knees splayed around the large steering wheel. She peers out the windshield, watching the limo pull out of the hotel's parking lot. Kirsten mutters under her breath.

"Nah, this is great," I say. I pick up another cassette: Barry Manilow. I place it back onto the dash. I realize where I am and who I am, a second-tier poet. I'm now watching the limo pull away, a silvery light shining off the door handles. I'm almost ready to scream, "Kirsten, they're getting away from us." But my sprightly gofer has the car in gear. We're now right behind the limo that holds the greatest child actor of all time, Hayley Mills, and the Academy Award winner from Industrial Light & Magic.

I chuckle with my head bowed. I close my eyes at this humorous moment—I, a poet, being hauled by a student in a wreck of a Honda to a five-course dinner that will be eaten, then passed through the system, forgotten. But the image has staying power: me in the clunker with the limo just in front, always in front; me, so hungry for fame at the beginning of my forties. My hair is black, my waist a spartan twenty-nine inches, my teeth a tad dull but still mine.

"Don't lose them," I joke to Kirsten.

"No way, José," she says. She grips the steering wheel with both hands. A blot of her breath fogs the glass; her head is nearly pressed to the windshield. The engine of her little Honda whines. She's determined to get me there, just seconds after that big-eight limo. She tells me that she'll wait for me to eat.

"What do you mean?" I ask. We're at a red light, then not at a red light. It's turned green. "You're not invited to the dinner?"

The bangles on her wrist make a merry music when she shifts gears. "Nope," she answers. "Don't worry."

But I do worry. I tell her so. I watch the cassettes on the dash do a jig as the Honda dips into a pothole.

She says she's just a volunteer, that I'm one of the filmmakers being honored.

"But my movie isn't any good," I tell her. I then add a sorrowful footnote: a boom was visible in one shot. Is that good filmmaking?

"Get out of here," she says as she bumps up a driveway and pulls the steering wheel to the right. "You're being modest."

"No, really," I counter. It's not a terrible film, as the lips are synched to the sound and the camera work is in focus. But an award-winning film? Questionable.

She says "Get out of here" a few more times when I tell her that I'm not going to make any more movies. I then reflect that it wouldn't be bad to be Barry Manilow for a while, say one year—then my money would be made. I could buy a ranch and outpace the trees in growing old.

Kirsten brakes right behind the limo. The chauffeur gets out and hurries to open the door for his passengers. But the valet at the restaurant—French, I see—has acted quickly, his gloved hand is already on the shiny door handle. Mr. Light & Magic gets out, followed by the organizer, then by Fake Hugh Grant, and, finally, Hayley Mills. She looks in our direction, a hand over her eyes from the brightness of the Honda's headlights. I have to wonder if the experience of fame makes you raise a hand to your face and say, "Alright already."

"Kirsten," I say, "I got to go." I touch her arm in appreciation and open the car door (myself), one leg and then the other hitting the sidewalk. We're both grinning. She knows it was unfair to have to ride in the cattle car but also knows that our short jaunt will be a story I will repeat. I turn and hustle up to the party until I'm on their heels. We of Filmlandia walk down the short red carpet that leads to the double doors. Unescorted and far from famous, I am wincing from the limelight.

I tip the guy holding the doors open five bucks. I tell him, "I'm with them."

THE DINING TABLE

WHEN I BEGAN TO SEND POEMS to literary magazines, I was timid, my arms like the wings of a penguin. My wingspan was short and, by all implications, my literary flight at ground level. I nearly begged numerous college and small-press magazines to accept my poems. If the answer was yes (the *Iowa Review* was the first to accept a poem, followed by *Poetry*, both in 1974), I did a jig around the oak dining table, the place where I wrote at all hours, the crumbs of my meals jigging, too, as I pounded my fist against the surface. I felt light and giddy, as if I had swallowed helium balloons, but eventually settled again at the oak table, which was Mission Style, from the 1910s. That round table was the center of a lot of meals. Plenty of beer and wine was consumed around it, as evidenced by the rings from all the mugs set on its surface. The table was small, about the size of someone extending his arms in a bear hug. Later, a pine leaf would be fitted into the table's center, to extend it, with a tablecloth hiding the mismatched plank.

But my earliest memory of this table? I was twenty, a third-year college student at Fresno State and enrolled in Speech. My assignment for the week was to read a scene from a play. I chose *Sorry, Wrong Number* by Lucille Fletcher and read it to Carolyn Oda, not then my wife, not then my girlfriend, but a neighbor who occasionally sent out the aroma of baked goods from her kitchen. One winter evening, I sat screaming out the lines of this one-act play while she sat with her face apparently empty of emotion, though behind the mask she was laughing freely at the comedy (Fletcher's play is supposed to be spine-tingling drama). Was anyone ever such a poor actor? She fed me a cookie and sent me on my way.

After Carolyn and I were married, I read my mail at this table. I made shopping lists there. I set a huge typewriter on it and wrote amidst the comings and goings of family, friends, and cats (Pippy, Groucho, and Corky). We were penguins—my wife, my daughter, and me—with short wingspans. We sat at the table, our wings coming together for a short prayer before dinner. "Pass the salt, please," I would say. Mariko, our daughter, would pat the salt toward me with her wing. "The ketchup, please," my wife would say. I would poke it over with my wing.

Birthdays were celebrated at this table, Thanksgiving, Christmas. Our friends were all penguins, though now and then a guest with the reach of an octopus would sit among us—a grappling thing from the deep! The table was where we did our taxes and computed our savings, licking the end of a pencil. It was where I wrote nineteen books—poetry, essays, and novels—and where I sat facing friends, our coffee cups steaming. I wrote condolence letters and birthday cards there. When I taught, I added up grades there at the end of the semester—you all get As.

That dining table is now in The Gary Soto Literary Museum. On it sits a manual typewriter, an electric typewriter, and an ancient laptop computer from pre-Internet days. Once a month I visit this old piece of furniture, which first belonged to my wife, then to the two of us, then to the three of us, our daughter doing her homework and science projects there. Now it belongs, like literature, to the public. I have placed my head on it many times, exhausted from getting words just right.

THE GARY SOTO LITERARY MUSEUM is located at Fresno City College, where I got my start as a poet in the spring of 1972. During the first stages of its construction, I asked a carpenter to build a small platform that would approximate our living room. I showed Greg, owner of the construction company, the museum plans by the designer, Jonathan Hirabayashi. Greg glanced at the blueprint, unfazed. The job was as complicated as taking off a door and sandpapering it. Still, the carpenter was curious about the space—a museum for books? I then described the purpose of the museum: to instill wonderment among the visitors, to say to kids that reading is important, to say to the city that literature matters, and to say that writers can emerge from a place like Fresno. I uttered all this casually.

When he expressed interest, I showed Greg the large metal chest of drawers where my poetry and prose manuscripts would be kept. I opened a drawer, which rolled out silently, not unlike the ones at the city morgue. I showed him the drawer where unsuccessful manuscripts would be kept, the dead ones, without a chance of reviving.

"This is where the books that never became books will be," I remarked. "They're not very good. They're just awful."

Greg fell silent. For a moment I thought his interest had waned, that I had gone on too long. But he'd been reflecting. He touched my shoulder and remarked, with heaviness in his heart, "Don't worry, Gary. I've done some bad jobs myself."

WHAT ARE POETS LIKE?

THEY ARE FUN, THEN NOT FUN. They are tall within themselves, but very short when applying for food stamps. If drunk, if male, they leak in public. If sober, they don't pee so much. They are made of air and words and may be a good date the first time around. When they sneeze, people step back. Dogs know them: they lick their chops for a dropped sandwich.

They are married, then not married. They are married again and then not married again. Soup they slurp with either hand, and bread they juggle from the toaster to a white plate. Butter? Butter they like, and fame they like if they don't have to travel too far.

Poets have jobs and they don't have jobs. They vote Democrat because they're smarter, though less educated, than Republicans. They have loans to pay off, hands that work, eyes that devour trees, noses that poke into other people's business. If they use the Cuisinart, they lick the blades for the frosting. Ouch, that hurts, but how sweet!

I'm a poet who started in dirt, who raised a green structure after the planting of bean plants. I was a poet with a fence and a poet with a hammer. I cut down weeds in fields and allowed soapsuds to climb my arms in a dirty car wash. Last week a dime rolled from my fingers and got away, but two pennies rolled back in my direction. Not bad—eight lost, but two

(I'll save them for later) to be placed on the dead eyelids, for sleep is eternity and the poetry inside us a song for the ages.

Poets worship in church and then don't worship—they just look around, marveling at the incense looping in the shape of a noose. They avoid police. They avoid order—they'll go when the light turns red. They speak to the sea and the sea speaks back. Crabs try to pick their pockets, and fish jump into their pockets for a ride home.

Love is an uneasy adventure, slippery as the unrolling of a condom. Some poets, but not all, love women, and some, but not all, love men. They are semigood at deception. They cover their tracks with a kick of sand. They father, they mother, and they push strollers from one block to the other. They call from rooms, "Honey, how do you spell 'fickle' in Estonian?"

Poets can't do anything but talk and rig words. If they tried to raise a scaffold, the world would be a much more dangerous place. If they had money, there would be a coin toss every five seconds. If they barbered heads, ears would scream from the floor. If they doctored, the living would jump into coffins and plead, "Nail it down good!"

What are poets like? They are difficult, then not difficult. They are strangers and then just plain strange. They are extremely jealous when they come in second.

They like France and Spain, and would even fly to China if they could return the same day. They are poor or very poor—these are the options they ponder as they stir potato soup on an old stove. They will scrape bark from a tree, and sniff it. They will hum a song, whittle a stick, and clock the speed of roaming clouds. They are lonely, this much we know. Dogs have come to them with the deepest felt of all greetings: a tongue rolling over knuckles in indisputable friendship. And like dogs, if you call them they will point to their chests and say, "You mean me?" If you nod your head, they will come running.

THE WINNING CROWD

I LIKE FOOTBALL BEST ON TELEVISION, in my own house, not at a sports bar where drinkers lift their eyes, the color of salmon eggs, when the crowd roars. I appreciate the ease of going to my own refrigerator, assessing what to eat and what to drink, and returning to the television, a Samsung, to watch what's there to watch. Wow, players in the air—no, players injured on the ground!

Then again, I don't like TV football at all. I abandoned the gladiator spectacle years ago when I discovered that there were more commercials than playing time, and that the audience on Sunday (and Monday and Thursday) was young and crude, with faces painted in team colors—or for the Igors of Raiders Nation sporting silvery spikes, shrunken heads, and fake (or real?) vomit. For some, every game is Halloween.

When my buddy David calls and says, "Let's get stupid," what he really means is let's uncork a bottle of wine, preferably Napa Valley red, and watch football players do their high-paid magic on television, then ask each other, "What's the score?" We'll eat a deep-dish Zachary's pizza, maybe get our veggies in the form of a Caesar salad, contemplate the meaning of life, then gaze up at the TV and ask, "Who's playing?"

While I don't really follow football, I have noticed that the crowds have been dressing down for years—slack jerseys hanging over wobbly guts and baseball caps worn backwards or sideways but never as they should be. When David got tickets to the last game of the season between the San Francisco 49ers and the Carolina Panthers, I decided to turn the sartorial tide, me against forty thousand other fans. The game itself didn't matter—both teams were out of the playoff picture—but I intended to dress to the nines.

The drive over the Bay Bridge was smooth and the parking pricy but equally smooth. A young woman wielding a lit wand waved us into our parking spot. We got out, both David and I complaining good-heartedly about the cold. The sky was gray as cement, and the wind was blowing off the bay, seagulls crying above. A plastic bag, white as a cloud, filled frantically with wind and was carried away by the gusts.

But I wasn't concerned about the weather. I had planned my wardrobe carefully, had examined every item in my closet—actually, a mirrored armoire with cubbyholes for shoes and a secret drawer for cufflinks. I was wearing a relatively new purchase from Adam of London, a tastefully designed wool suit that's chocolate-colored with very faint pinstripes. In another life I might have been one of the Rolling Stones, circa 1965, when English band members dressed in three-piece suits, totally mod, totally groovy. And on my feet? Polished black leather high-tops, mirror bright at the tips. My hat? A black felt Borsalino, with a feather in its band. It would insulate my brain and conceal my receding hairline—a nice touch.

But you wouldn't have noticed my suit because it was hidden beneath a long, maroon overcoat made by my wife in the late 1980s, when shoulder pads were all the rage and, in this case, nearly as big as pillows. The thick wool falls to my knees and, because of its heft, wearing the coat is a workout in itself. The buttons are football-shaped, made of polished walnut. The label inside says, "For my Sweetie." That's me, and there I was meandering through the parking lot, thirty minutes before kickoff, receiving stares from all the tailgaters—would-be jocks, or former jocks, or just fans out for a good time.

"Dude! Dude!" a bearded chap shouted. "You look hella strange." This fan was holding a beer in one hand, a flaccid hotdog in the other—the frankfurter, I noticed, was nearly slipping from its holster of a bun and had a little yellow dot of mustard at the end.

"Go Niners," I offered with a clenched fist, ignoring his taunt. I gave him a peace sign and a grin as I ducked through the smoke wafting from his hibachi. I could endure any insult to my attire, by far the sharpest within miles. And hey, I might have said, "Look! Gold cufflinks on the T.M.Lewin 100 percent pima cotton shirt I bought in London." And over the weenies you're flaying on the grill, I could have touched my scented throat and added, "Only the best—Le Male cologne."

I shared more peace signs, then double-barrel peace signs, as I passed row after row of tipsy partygoers, and bore with dignity the stares, the quips ("Oh, check out grandpa!"), the sound of beer cans crushed in wrench-like hands (what had I done?), and even a shower of peanuts.

"You're causing trouble," David smirked.

"True," I agreed, dusting my sleeve of a clinging peanut. "A well-dressed man will do that."

At my age (late fifties), you seldom get a chance to cause trouble, unless you lean on your horn and yell at another driver, "Hey, butt-face, use your turn signal!" Then speed away, eyes in the rearview mirror. Or unless on a lovely Saturday you are pulled over for rolling through a stop sign, and you furrow your brow and mutter as you sign the ticket, "I'm a naughty old man."

We made our way through security, where I had to unbutton my coat for a quick pat down and permit security's peek into my paper bag: two turkey sandwiches prepared by my wife, along with two Fuji apples, two bottles of water, and a small vial of antibacterial hand sanitizer. The bottled water was confiscated—no liquids allowed.

David had bought our tickets through Goldstar, an online retailer that offers 50 to 70 percent off the list price. We like a bargain, not to mention entertainment. But our seats were located in a section far from the gridiron action, and at such an angle that we were guaranteed stiff necks by halftime.

"Follow me," I told David, who was shelling a couple of the peanuts he'd caught during the last barrage. I led the way to the lower level, now and then touching the brim of my hat as some fan smiled and pointed at me, the ambassador of good taste. One of the vendors, a young guy with a bluish tattoo on his neck, stopped his sales pitch. Excited, he sang, "You a hit man! You a hit man! Like in the movies, huh!"

"Young man, you have me all wrong," I answered, slipping my right hand into my coat pocket. "I'm nothing more than a 49er faithful."

The vendor shaped his hand into a pistol and I played along, my own hand rising pistol-shaped from my coat pocket, the trigger of my thumb pulled back. "Put yours back, buddy," I warned, "and just walk away slowly." He smiled and moved along, evidently unwilling to risk an encounter with this OG, the bags of peanuts dangling from his fist.

We approached a female security guard in a bright yellow windbreaker. She had been barking at a boy standing at the railing, but when she spotted me the boy vanished from her thoughts. Who was this gentleman coming toward her? She brushed her blondish hair behind an ear and literally licked her lips. Was her rusty ship about to find its home port? She smiled, displaying a wad of bluish gum near her molars, and said, "Oh, my daddy! Who are you?" She eyed me up and down, then rotated her attention to David. He was dressed in an L.L.Bean hooded jacket, with a sweater beneath it, jeans that were pale at the knees, a baseball cap (sun-washed from hours of tennis), and leather deck shoes—decent garb but certainly not the dress of a dandy. Her gaze returned to me. Ever the gent, I greeted her by touching my hat brim and remarked, "Pretty cold, huh?" I would have rubbed my hands together, but I was still holding our lunch.

"Are you a manager?" she asked, her jaw working the bluish gum to the other side of her mouth.

"You mean an executive for the team?" I asked. My gaze floated to the luxury boxes that rimmed part of the stadium.

"Yeah," she answered. She also looked up at the luxury boxes.

I wagged my head.

"A scout?" she wondered, furrowing her brow.

I wagged my head a second time. "No, just a student of the game," I told her. At that, I dabbed my nose with a handkerchief, feeling intensely disappointed that it wasn't monogrammed "GS." But it was 100 percent cotton (although *hecho en* India) and white as a surrender flag.

"You're good," she answered in return. "Sit wherever you want." She was aware that we possessed tickets for the nosebleed section, but since the game was not a sellout and I was a different kind of man, in full regalia, she let us pass.

David was impressed, and said so. "Dang, Gary." He offered to carry our lunch, which in my new role seemed a burden. Even I had to admit that carrying a paper bag with a stain on the bottom didn't suit my attire.

I was a man from another era, but which era was that? Pick a decade before the 1960s, any decade, and almost any professional sport, including boxing. The public dressed differently then. If you look at game photos from the 1940s, you see that the men—and women—wore suits and hats. By all appearances those fans were more civil. There was no conglomerate called Raiders Nation, no young men shirtless in the cold and beating their chests like tom-toms. Was there shouting? Probably. But when the referee's call went against their team, those fans certainly did not shout such vindictive phrases as the modern, all-purpose "You mother#&@@@!" Were these 1940s fans better people? Probably not. Still, the image evokes a time when a sporting society knew the cursive weave of a Windsor knot.

We took our seats in row G. From this vantage point we could see vapor rising off the hulking defensemen near the sideline. Some had their hands on their hips, others were down on one knee, as if in prayer. The energetic cheerleaders were doing what they do best: kicking up their legs and spanking their pom-poms together. The electronic scoreboards were illuminated, brighter than reality itself. Above the scoreboards whirled seagulls, and above them, a single plane pulled a Budweiser banner.

Beer, I thought. Although it was only one in the afternoon, I was ready for fortification. I rose. I cinched the belt of my overcoat and told David, "I'll be back." I climbed the concrete steps. The female security guard pitchforked her eyes with splayed fingers, then pointed those fingers (tattooed, I noted) at me. She mouthed silently, "I got eyes for you."

Flirty thing, I thought.

I had my sights on two overpriced beers. For a second, I'd considered wine but knew it probably wouldn't be decent for the price and would certainly be meager, maybe only three inches of red in a clear plastic cup. As I sidled up to the beer station—a wagon-like kitchen on wheels—I received a pat on the shoulder. I turned to see a guy with a sunflower seed shell pasted to his front tooth grinning at me. He was drunk, and he was sloppy. His shoelaces were undone and sodden, probably from dragging in the urinals. "You look funny," he remarked.

He could have been wittier, or at least specific in what he meant by "funny." He could have spoken of the quality of the wool in my overcoat, or remarked on my shoes, particularly the left one, which squeaked like a mouse with each step. Or he could have pointed at the tidy knot of my tie, purchased from Seaward & Stearn during my last romp in the Cotswolds (2009, as I remember). Better yet, he could have kept his hands to himself. Were bacteria now squirming on my shoulder?

He spoke again: "You're, like, funny." The sunflower seed shell spurted from his mouth and onto the ground between us.

Ugly, I thought, real ugly. I realized that I had to meet this guy on his own terms!

"You talkin' to me?" I asked, imagining the question as uttered by Robert De Niro in *Taxi Driver*. But my attempt lacked fire—it should have come out with a curl of flames. I took a deep breath, ready to repeat my line, but the fellow was done with me. He turned away, hooking a thumb at me. "He's a funny dude!" he yelled before disappearing among the other 49er jerseys, shoelaces dragging.

I would have brooded on this encounter except for the gust of wind that nearly tipped off my hat. I remembered who I was: a gentleman for the day.

I acquired our beverage of choice, Blue Moon wheat beer, and thanked the person behind the bar with a two-dollar tip. As I navigated back to our seats, a tide of foamy beer dampened my knuckles. I was forced to stop and sip a little of the overpriced brew. I soon stopped again, this time to accept a telephone number from the security guard in the windbreaker. Her name was Elena and she lived in a 650 prefix (not far, maybe Pacifica or San Mateo). She went through her routine, pitchforking two splayed fingers at her eyes, then pointing these fingers at me.

"I get it," I said. "You got your eyes on me."

She smiled, showing me the backs of her molars, where a wad of chewing gum seemed to have changed from blue to green. She lifted a hand to an ear and mimicked, "Call me."

Moving carefully down the aisle toward my seat, I mouthed: "I got my eyes on you too." She'd allowed us to sit in a better section. I had to give her something.

"You're like a dream," she said, fading flower in a bright yellow windbreaker.

Finally, I returned with the goods: two hefty beers. When I sat down my face was pink. She's very sweet, I thought, and glanced back at the security guard. She was clapping her mittened hands at a boy, urging him to get away from the rail.

"Good work, Gary," David offered. We nudged our plastic glasses together and took judicious sips—at eight dollars a cup we had to make this beer last!

We proceeded to witness the destruction on the field. I reached for my hat every now and then whenever the wind, a bully with cold breath, would nearly knock it off my head. David and I talked about Hemingway's *A Moveable Feast*, a memoir set in Paris during the 1920s. Although Hemingway and his first wife, Hadley, are supposed to be young and starving, they seem to sit down to a good meal with lots of quality wine on every page. Hemingway had been a reporter then, and, like any other young writer, he was observant, conceited, passionate about his craft, and busily searching for a subject, for a purpose, and for a few coins to continue living in Paris. During his time there Hemingway had visited Ezra Pound, James Joyce, Fitzgerald—

A big roar from the crowd turned our attention to the game. The 49ers had just scored a touchdown on a short pass to Crabtree, their premier receiver, who sprinted effortlessly into the end zone. We followed the crowd and stood up, clapped, and exchanged high fives.

We sat back down. "Exciting," I said, then reached into the bag for the antibacterial hand sanitizer and squirted a glob into my palm. David refused the life-saving potion. I brought out our turkey sandwiches, noticing that my wife had given us the works: smoked gouda cheese with out-of-season heirloom tomatoes. So thoughtful, I thought, and sighed.

When another roar erupted, I looked back onto the field. A Carolina player had fumbled. I took a bite of my diminishing sandwich, wiped my mouth, and asked David, "We're in the lead, right?"

"Right," he answered. He lowered his face and began plowing away on his turkey sandwich. He nodded his head in appreciation.

It was nearing the end of the quarter, and I considered ending my pretense. It had been fun assuming the role of another person from another time, but I was done pushing buttons. Other people, however, weren't done with me. Over my shoulder, I heard someone call, "Hey, pimp." A flung Frito ticked against the back of a nearby seat.

I had been examining my apple, its spotted surface a sign that it had been grown organically (ah, my dear wife—she's too perfect). After he hollered "pimp" twice more, I looked up and answered, "No, dear fellow, it's 'Pimp Daddy.' Let's get it right." Then, squirrel-like, I took a small bite of my apple, then another. Two more taps of Fritos against my back—the troublemaker's aim was getting better.

The guy giggled and gave the Igor next to him a high five.

A few minutes later, someone called, "Hey, gangster!"

"Gangster," his sidekick hollered, using his hands as a megaphone.

More high fives from the Igors in the rows behind, followed now by a shower of peanuts. But I had my fedora to protect my head and my coat as body armor. I was immune from the barrages, both words and projectiles, which now included ice cubes and jelly beans from the section above us.

I was called gangster and pimp, preacher man and banker man, big daddy and small daddy. One snarky troublemaker called me George W. Bush—boy, did that hurt!

I remained gentlemanly throughout and committed to my lunch. A bunch of grapes, a surprise treat found at the bottom of the bag, was sweetening my breath after a turkey sandwich. But the yokels couldn't find another distraction, which made me think that watching football isn't really about the game in front of you but about the opportunity to drink and vent. Was this all about working out anger? Possibly.

David huddled around his turkey sandwich. "I knew this was going to happen," he said. We then revisited 1920s Paris, Hemingway's cold apartments, and the cafés where he wrote and read and listened to others in simple declarative sentences. We were talking about how he had given Ezra Pound a few boxing lessons when once again a roar made us look toward the field.

"A fumble!" David cried.

"Our bad or theirs?" I asked.

"Their bad," David answered. He then complained that if the 49ers had won last week's game they would've had a wild-card spot. Now they were playing only for hometown pride, doing their best to entertain the fans.

Of course, I had been putting on my own kind of entertainment. I was different; I was a dandy. There had been a purpose to this. I could have been an Aztec warrior in full costume, with feathers on my rump and bells made from dried seeds on my ankles. I could have been a piper from the Scottish Highlands charging about in a kilt. I could have been a cape-swinging matador in the wrong sort of stadium. The odd part was how my unusual attire invited attention, then anger, then abuse for being different.

I visited the men's room—more looks. I visited the microbrewery—looks again, this time from drunken men with those salmon-egg eyes. I passed three cops, sneers creeping from the corners of their mouths.

I would've bought a horseshoe pretzel, except that two *vato locos* were snorting at me. I did an about-face and made my way back to my seat. I had suddenly embraced common sense.

"It's fun, huh?" David asked. Fog was rolling overhead, and he was shivering from the cold.

"Tons," I answered. I stuffed my hands into my pockets and felt around for a pack of gum. I offered a stick to David, then folded one into my mouth. I examined Elena's telephone number again. It had been written, I realized, on a scrap of a Supercuts business card. Was that her day job? Or was she a customer herself? She was in her late forties, fit and good at her work (no one dared lean against the rail), and, by all appearances, a nice person. I sighed, dropping the card onto the ground. After all, I was a married man.

The game was over before the fourth quarter. The Panthers played more like kittens than the sleek cats displayed on their helmets. David and I had seen enough. I touched fingers with a few fans as I walked up the concrete steps, a celebrity, a TV actor, a rocker (was that Carlos Santana?), a disgraced politician, perhaps an owner checking on how the crowd was enjoying itself. I was disappointed to find that Elena wasn't at her station. We could have done that pitchfork business, and I could have lifted my hand to my ear, suggesting the call that would never be made.

"You remember where we're parked?" David asked after our spiraling walk down the ramp.

I looked skyward, sniffed, and pulled up my collar. The plane with the Budweiser banner was receding in the gray sky, its job done. At least one entire section of fans was most suitably fortified. But the seagulls were still circling and plastic bags swirled from gusts of wind.

"Piece of cake," I answered, suddenly Sherlock Holmes. I looked down at the ground, a bloodhound of sorts, and discovered a route. We followed a trail of beer cans, cigarette butts, dropped hotdogs, plastic forks and knives, torn tickets, scattered popcorn and Cracker Jacks, and largish puddles of what I hoped was spilled beer but understood was urine.

I had made friends with the winning crowd.

Carolyn Soto

ABOUT THE AUTHOR

GARY SOTO began writing poetry in 1973 and published his first book, *The Elements of San Joaquin* in 1977. Since then, he has published twelve other full-length collections, including *New and Selected Poems*, a 1995 finalist for both the Los Angeles Times Book Prize and the National Book Award. His most recent poetry collection is *Sudden Loss of Dignity* (2013). His poem "Oranges" is the most anthologized poem in contemporary literature. The Gary Soto Literary Museum is located at Fresno City College, where he got his start as a poet. With his wife, Carolyn, he lives in Berkeley, California.